THE ULTIMATE
ATLANTA BRAVES
TRIVIA BOOK

A Collection of Amazing Trivia Quizzes
and Fun Facts for Die-Hard Braves Fans!

Ray Walker

CONTENTS

INTRODUCTION

Obviously, you're inspired by your favorite team. In this case, the team in lights is none other than the Braves, one of the original franchises in the National League, and surely one of the best ever in the entire glorious history of Major League Baseball (although archrival New York Mets fans might want to argue over your claim just a bit).

The city of Atlanta, "the Big Peach," has long been filled with winning pro teams: the Atlanta Hawks in the NBA, the Falcons in the NFL, and now Atlanta United FC in MLS. Coca-Cola, CNN, Delta Airlines, and UPS make the city even more dynamic.

But your Atlanta Braves are extra special. There's no place in the world to play hard ball like their unique home stadium, Truist Park, a mere 10 miles from Downtown Atlanta, filled with 41,084 tomahawk-chopping and screaming Braves fans.

Next year, the Braves will celebrate 150 years of existence at (or near!) the peak of the baseball world, and you'll be there, armed with all the trivia and fun facts on their colorful players, big signings and trades, and the incredible emotional highs and lows of a world championship team. The Braves have had more than their fair share and not just the team's historic late-season collapse in 2011. But we all must overcome, and there are many more merrier moments like the last World Series win in 1995 (along with a near-miss in 1992).

Clearly, you may use the book as you wish. Each chapter contains 20 quiz questions that offer a mix of multiple-choice and true-false formats along with an answer key (Don't worry, it's on a separate page!) and a selection of 10 "Did You Know? " facts about the team.

For the record, the information and stats in this book are current up to the beginning of 2020. The Braves will surely break more records and win many more awards as the seasons march on, so keep this in mind when you're watching the next game with your friends. You never quite know: someone could suddenly start a conversation with the phrase "Did you know…?" And you'll be ready.

CHAPTER 1:

ORIGINS & HISTORY

QUIZ TIME!

1. The Atlanta Braves originated in a city far from their current home in Georgia. Where did they start in 1871?

    a. Baltimore
    b. Boston
    c. Cleveland
    d. Milwaukee

2. In what year did the team move to Braves Field in the aforementioned city?

    a. 1900
    b. 1907
    c. 1915
    d. 1922

3. The Braves club is the oldest continuous franchise in the history of professional baseball.

    a. True
    b. False

4. The only other professional team in existence as long as the Braves, the Chicago Cubs, stopped playing for two consecutive years in 1871. Why?

   a. The Spanish Flu Pandemic
   b. The Great Chicago Fire
   c. The Great Depression
   d. The Stock Market Crash

5. Before they became the Braves, what was the team's first official name?

   a. Bears
   b. Cougars
   c. Red Stockings
   d. Whales

6. The original team was called various other names, including the Red Caps. Which of the following was another?

   a. Aboriginals
   b. Beaneaters
   c. Beantowners
   d. Bombers

7. In 1901, what event seriously damaged the team's chances?

   a. New American League entry in the same city
   b. President McKinley's shooting
   c. Severe heat wave
   d. Typhoid fever outbreak

8. The Braves put together a "miracle" season in 1914,

coming back from last place on July 4 to win the pennant and sweep the Series. Who was their final victim?

a. Brooklyn Giants
b. Chicago Cubs
c. Philadelphia A's
d. St. Louis Cardinals

9. Which player did owner Emil Fuchs sign to try to right the Braves' ship in 1935?

a. Babe Ruth
b. Christy Mathewson
c. Hank Greenberg
d. Lou Gehrig

10. Unfortunately, the Braves played their worst ball ever that year and recorded the second-worst season in NL history. Which team had the worst-ever NL percentage in 1899?

a. Chicago Black Stockings
b. Cleveland Spiders
c. New York Mets
d. Washington Senators

11. Shortly before moving to Milwaukee, the Braves just missed playing in an all-Boston World Series when Cleveland beat the Red Sox in a one-game playoff. What was the year?

a. 1944
b. 1946
c. 1948
d. 1950

12. In 1950, Sam "Jet" Jethro became the oldest player, at 32, to win Rookie of the Year when he broke the color barrier. Who was his African-American roomie who broke the National Basketball Association's color barrier with the Celtics the same year?

    a. Chuck Cooper
    b. Bob Cousy
    c. Sonny Hertzberg
    d. Brady Walker

13. One reason for the Braves moving to Milwaukee was that they weren't the most popular team in Boston anymore. Which Red Sox player boosted that Boston team's rise?

    a. Dom DiMaggio
    b. Johnny Pesky
    c. Ted Williams
    d. Carl Yastrzemski

14. After eight decades in Beantown, what did Bostonians call the sad day the Braves moved?

    a. Black Friday
    b. Braves Day of Reckoning
    c. Depression Day
    d. Doomsday

15. The Braves had a top farm club, the Brewers, in Milwaukee in 1953. Which other team, owned by Bill Veeck, wanted to move to Milwaukee that year?

    a. Cincinnati Reds
    b. Kansas City A's

c. St. Louis Browns

d. St. Louis Cardinals

16. Milwaukee went crazy for the Braves upon their arrival, setting the NL attendance record at that time. How many fans did they draw in 1953?

a. 1.42 million

b. 1.54 million

c. 1.65 million

d. 1.8 million

17. Sluggers Henry Aaron and Eddie Mathews combined for a total of 1,226 dingers while playing for the Braves. How many of those were hit while they played in Milwaukee?

a. 740

b. 785

c. 850

d. 975

18. In 1957, the Braves busted their way to their first World Series victory in more than 40 years. Who pitched three complete-game wins to shut down the Yankees?

a. Bob Buhl

b. Lew Burdette

c. Johnny Sain

d. Warren Spahn

19. In 1962, the Braves were sold to a Chicago-based group who then shopped the team to a city with a larger TV audience. Who was the Atlanta mayor behind a new stadium to snag the Braves?

a. Ivan Allen Jr.

b. Jane Fonda

c. Roy LeCraw

d. Ted Turner

20. In 1969, Atlanta won the first-ever NL West pennant and then lost in the NLCS. What was the nickname of the team that shut Atlanta down?

a. Crazy Cubbies

b. Ever-Exciting Expos

c. Miracle Mets

d. We-Are-Family Pirates

QUIZ ANSWERS

1. B – Boston

2. C – 1915

3. A – True

4. B – The Great Chicago Fire

5. C – Red Stockings

6. B – Beaneaters

7. A – New American League entry in the same city (Boston)

8. C – Philadelphia A's

9. A – Babe Ruth

10. B – Cleveland Spiders

11. C – 1948

12. A – Chuck Cooper

13. C – Ted Williams

14. A – Black Friday

15. C – St. Louis Browns

16. D – 1.8 million

17. C – 850

18. B – Lew Burdette

19. A – Ivan Allen Jr.

20. C – Miracle Mets

DID YOU KNOW?

1. In 1886, the Boston Beaneaters (predecessors of the Braves) had a hurler named Charles "Old Hoss" Radbourn. The first photographic record of the middle finger, shown by Hoss, is prominent in the team picture that year.

2. The Boston franchise played at Braves Field, now known as Nickerson Field at Boston University, from 1915 to 1952.

3. The first unqualified sweep in the early history of the modern World Series happened when the underdog Braves beat the Philadelphia Athletics, managed by Connie Mack, in 1907.

4. When Braves Field opened in 1915, it featured a novelty: Public transport brought fans directly to the park's doorstep.

5. In 1935, Braves owner Fuchs brought in Babe Ruth, promising him an eventual managing job. But his performance, especially fielding, became so bad that three pitchers threatened to strike if the Babe played.

6. In 1948, the Braves won the pennant behind the brilliant pitching of Warren Spahn and Johnny Sain and almost nobody else. A Boston writer penned a poem: "Spahn, Sain, then pray for rain."

7. Sam "Jet" Jethro blasted through the color barrier with the Boston Braves in 1950 and became the oldest NL Rookie of

the Year at 32. His line was a .273 BA, 101 runs, 58 RBI, and 35 stolen bags—the most by a Brave since Hap Myers grabbed 57 in 1913.

8. The Braves became the first team to seek success in another city—namely Milwaukee—in 1953. Four other teams followed in five years: the Philadelphia Athletics, St. Louis Browns, Brooklyn Dodgers, and New York Giants.

9. Despite Aaron smashing 44 dingers and 130 RBI while Spahn posted a .767 winning mark in 1963, the Braves finished in the league's second division for the first time in Milwaukee.

10. After the Braves' 1966 move to Atlanta, fans had to be happy with Hank Aaron's increased production, despite the team's mediocrity. At the time, Atlanta Stadium was nicknamed "The Launching Pad."

CHAPTER 2:

WHAT'S IN A NAME?

QUIZ TIME!

1. Which of the following was NOT another name used to refer to the Braves during their long history?

   a. Bees
   b. Cowboys
   c. Doves
   d. Rustlers

2. What's the previous name of the Braves' current ballpark, Truist Park?

   a. SunTan Park
   b. SunTrust Park
   c. True Lies Park
   d. Turner Field

3. In which Georgia county is Truist Park situated?

   a. Cherokee
   b. Cobb
   c. Peach
   d. Rockdale

4. The Braves normally play their spring training games in CoolToday Park in Florida. In what city?

   a. Fort Lauderdale
   b. Miami
   c. North Port
   d. St. Petersburg

5. What TV network was responsible for the Braves earning the nickname "America's Team" from the 1970s to 2007?

   a. CBS
   b. HBO
   c. NBC
   d. TBS

6. Which company is currently the principal owner of the Braves franchise?

   a. AOL Time Warner
   b. Liberty Media
   c. Pulseworks
   d. Turner Broadcasting

7. The 1898 Boston Beaneaters team set a record for wins (102) that stood for a century. What was the nickname of the two stars, Hugh Duffy and Tommy McCarthy, at the time?

   a. The Beaneating Basestealers
   b. The Heavenly Twins
   c. The Hugh and Tommy Show
   d. The Sliders

8. The Braves secured their name in 1912 when President John Ward called owner James Gaffney one of the "braves" of New York City's political machine. What was the organization's name?

    a. The Bull Moose Party
    b. The New Deal Coalition
    c. The Socialist Party
    d. Tammany Hall

9. In 1923, Judge Emil Fuchs bought the Braves and tried to bring back one of his longtime friends, a former pitching great. Who was he?

    a. Christy Mathewson
    b. Cy Williams
    c. Irish Meusel
    d. Hack Miller

10. When the Braves beat the indomitable Yankees in the 1957 Series, which of the following players was NOT featured in the New York lineup?

    a. Mickey Mantle
    b. Phil Rizzuto
    c. Whitey Ford
    d. Yogi Berra

11. Braves fans in 1959 hoped for a Series pitting Milwaukee against another team a mere 75 miles down the freeway, but it was not to be. Which team was it?

    a. Chicago Cubs
    b. Chicago White Sox

c. Cleveland Indians

d. Minnesota Twins

12. Which expansion team helped pad the Braves' win total in the early 1960s?

a. Houston Colt .45s

b. Los Angeles Angels

c. Seattle Supersonics

d. Washington Senators

13. Who is the only Brave to have played in all three cities (Boston, Milwaukee, and Atlanta)?

a. Del Rice

b. Eddie Mathews

c. Joey Jay

d. Bobby Thomson

14. Hank Aaron put up prodigious home run numbers. But in 1973, two other Atlanta sluggers crushed 40 or more. Which of these was NOT one of them?

a. Darrell Evans

b. Davey Johnson

c. Dusty Baker

15. "Hammerin' Hank" Aaron broke former Brave Babe Ruth's career HR record on national TV and in front of the Atlanta faithful, on April 8, 1974. What was opposing pitcher Al Downing's team?

a. Houston Astros

b. Los Angeles Dodgers

c. New York Mets

d. Pittsburgh Pirates

16. Considered one of the best-ever Braves, for which state (besides Georgia) is Dale Murphy a Hall-of-Famer?

a. Delaware

b. North Carolina

c. Oregon

d. Washington

17. Outstanding Braves outfielder Andruw Jones tracked the Atlanta outfield for more than a decade. Where is he originally from?

a. Aruba

b. Cuba

c. Curaçao

d. Dominican Republic

18. Chipper Jones got his nickname from his coach and dad as "a chip off the old block." What was his real first name?

a. Lanny

b. Larry

c. Louis

d. Lancaster

19. Braves iconic manager Bobby Cox holds the all-time MLB record for most ejections (158, plus three more in the postseason). Who was the previous record-holder?

a. Billy Martin

b. Casey Stengel

c. Sweet Lou Piniella

d. Tug McGraw

20. Phil Niekro was the last MLB pitcher to finish with more than 20 wins and 20 losses (he was 21-20 as a Brave in 1979). What was his nickname?

a. Knucksie

b. Knucklehead

c. The Grand Poohbah

d. Wild Thing

QUIZ ANSWERS

1. B – Cowboys

2. B – SunTrust Park

3. B – Cobb

4. C – North Port

5. D – TBS

6. B – Liberty Media

7. B – The Heavenly Twins

8. D – Tammany Hall

9. A – Christy Mathewson

10. B – Phil Rizzuto

11. B – Chicago White Sox

12. A – Houston Colt .45s

13. B – Eddie Mathews

14. C – Dusty Baker

15. B – Los Angeles Dodgers

16. C – Oregon

17. C – Curaçao

18. B – Larry

19. D – Tug McGraw

20. A – Knucksie

DID YOU KNOW?

1. Cuban Zoilo Casanova Versalles arrived in Atlanta after winning a couple of Gold Gloves as a Twin. Fans loved his name, but his .191 batting average not so much.

2. Rowland Johnie Office is probably more renowned for sharing left field duties with Hank Aaron in 1974 than his actual playing ability.

3. Dick "Mule" Dietz had one fine season (1973) as a backup first baseman with the Braves. He's arguably most famous for being hit by a Don Drysdale pitch as a Giant, but not being given first because the umpire ruled that he didn't try to avoid the delivery.

4. Unfortunately, Jim Panther couldn't turn his name into pitching ability with the Braves: He sported a 7.63 ERA in 30 Atlanta innings in 1973.

5. Wenty Ford was born in the Bahamas and spent his entire career (of four games) with Atlanta. He claimed to have three pitching speeds: "Slow, slower, and stop."

6. Catcher Biff Pocoroba played in Atlanta all of his 10-year career (1975-1984). What's better is that Biff is his real name, not a nickname.

7. Blue Moon Odom pitched alongside Catfish Hunter with the illustrious Oakland A's when owner Charlie Finley "forced" some players to adopt nicknames. Odom only had 10 sad starts for Atlanta.

8. Another Brave called Trench Davis made three plate appearances in 1987 as a pinch-hitter. Alas, he didn't reach base. And his first name Trench really appeared on his birth certificate.

9. Gaylord Perry pitched for one season (1981) in Atlanta and posted a reasonable 3.94 ERA in 150 innings. He eventually found his way into the Hall of Fame.

10. Cletis "Clete" Boyer (1967-1971) and Charlie Spikes (1979-1980) also donned Braves uniforms. All seven boys in Clete's Missouri family of 14 children played pro ball.

CHAPTER 3:

FAMOUS QUOTES

QUIZ TIME!

1. One well-known manager said, "I feel very fortunate to have broken in with the Milwaukee Braves organization." Who was he?

   a. Bobby Cox
   b. Lum Harris
   c. Russ Nixon
   d. Joe Torre

2. Matt Kemp once said, "Somebody had asked me how it was to be in Atlanta, and I said that Atlanta had always been known as a Braves city, a baseball _____."

   a. Capital
   b. Mecca
   c. Oasis
   d. Town

3. In what way did Theo Epstein say the Red Sox were trying to transform themselves to be more like the Braves?

a. You can almost count on never losing.

b. You can almost count on tasting 50 types of food when you visit the ballpark.

c. You can almost count on the postseason every year.

d. You can almost count on three million fans every year.

4. A certain player who grew up only hours from Atlanta rooting for the Braves was suddenly traded by the A's to his hometown team in 2005. His dream to play for the "legendary" Bobby Cox came true. Who was it?

a. Joe Blanton

b. Santiago Casilla

c. Tim Hudson

d. Barry Zito

5. Matt Lanter quipped, "If I wasn't a/an _____, I probably would've tried to get a job with the Braves."

a. Actor

b. CEO

c. Ditch digger

d. Executive

6. When Brian Baumgartner was a kid in the '80s, he swears it was tough to go to Braves games because they usually piled up 100 losses a year. Which players turned it around for him in '91?

a. Nixon and Belliard

b. Petry and Avery

c. Sanders and Pendleton

d. Smoltz and Glavine

7. Which Braves pitcher said this in 1991: "I think I'm better when I'm fired up out there and real aggressive."?

   a. Steve Avery
   b. Juan Berenguer
   c. Tom Glavine
   d. Randy St. Claire

8. Which Braves owner was "very passionate and did whatever it took to do something good, and eventually made money"?

   a. William C. Bartholomay
   b. Louis R. Perini
   c. Ted Turner
   d. Arthur H. Soden

9. Yankees scout Pat Gillick was trying "to land an 18-year-old strapping first baseman from Blanco, Texas, population 200." His name was Willie Upshaw, and only one other scout knew of him. Who?

   a. Mel Didier (Oakland A's)
   b. Fred Petersen (Red Sox)
   c. Al LaMacchia (Braves)
   d. Don Williams (Padres)

10. Which pitcher said his years as a Card were the best of his baseball life, but he respected everybody with Atlanta, "an awfully fine organization," a place where he still lives today?

   a. Al Hrabosky
   b. Charles "Silver" King

c. Bruce Sutter

d. Slim Sallee

11. Chuck Tanner exclaimed, "If you don't like the way the Atlanta Braves are playing, then you don't like _____."

a. Anything

b. Baseball

c. Sports

d. Yourself

12. Which self-made model proclaimed, "No one ever taught me how to shave; no one ever sat down to watch a Braves game with me."?

a. Tyson Beckford

b. Giselle Bundchen

c. Sean O'Pry

d. Kip Pardue

13. Manager Bobby Cox said about one of his players: "I can't say enough about the kid. It's fun to watch him play. He's got _____ written all over his face."

a. Baseball

b. Braves

c. Runs

d. Winner

14. Which Braves announcer was responsible for saying, "The bases are loaded, and Jack McKeon wishes he was as well."?

a. Chip Caray

b. Harry "Skip" Caray Jr.

c. Jon Sciambi

d. Joe Simpson

15. The famous call, "Fly ball, left field, _____ on the run... Yes, yes, yes, yes! The Atlanta Braves have given you a championship!" was also made by the elder Caray. Who was the 1995 outfielder who hauled in the final out?

    a. (Mike) Devereaux

    b. (Marquis) Grissom

    c. (David) Justice

    d. (Dwight) Smith

16. Which sympathetic teammate once quipped, "Trying to sneak a fastball past Hank Aaron is like trying to sneak the sunrise past a rooster."?

    a. Joe Adcock

    b. Alvin Dark

    c. Sal Maglie

    d. Eddie Mathews

17. The Braves recently removed a sign shown in front of Truist Park due to racial insensitivity towards Native Americans. What was the sign's previous slogan?

    a. "Atlanta's Burnin' Down"

    b. "Chop On"

    c. "Chop Suey"

    d. "Do The Brave"

18. Which Braves batter said this: "The triple is the most exciting play in baseball. Home runs win a lot of games,

but I never understood why the fans are so obsessed with them."?

a. Hank Aaron
b. Chipper Jones
c. Eddie Mathews
d. Dale Murphy

19. Hammerin' Hank once explained, "Guessing what the pitcher is going to throw is 80% of being a successful hitter. The other 20% is just _____."

a. Control
b. Execution
c. Passion
d. Patience

20. Aaron admitted, "It took me __ years to get three thousand hits in baseball. I did it in one afternoon on the golf course."

a. 13
b. 15
c. 17
d. 19

QUIZ ANSWERS

1. D – Joe Torre

2. D – Town

3. C – You can almost count on the postseason every year.

4. C – Tim Hudson

5. A – Actor

6. D – Smoltz and Glavine

7. A – Steve Avery

8. C – Ted Turner

9. C – Al LaMacchia (Braves)

10. C – Bruce Sutter

11. B – Baseball

12. D – Kip Pardue

13. D – Winner

14. B – Harry "Skip" Caray Jr.

15. B – (Marquis) Grissom

16. A – Joe Adcock

17. B – "Chop On"

18. A – Hank Aaron

19. B – Execution

20. C – 17

DID YOU KNOW?

1. In the 1970s, Aaron ruminated, "On the field, blacks have been able to be super giants. But, once our playing days are over, this is the end of it and we go back to the back of the bus again."

2. Clearly, the pitcher was at a decided disadvantage against Hank. "The pitcher has got only a ball. So the percentage in weapons is in my favor and I let the fellow with the ball do the fretting," he reasoned.

3. The media were more difficult than the game, according to Aaron: "People were not ready to accept me as a baseball player. The easiest part of that whole thing, chasing the Babe's record, was playing the game itself. The hardest thing was after the game was over, dealing with the press. They could never understand."

4. John Smoltz showed he was as good at math as any Braves fan: "We just have to remember that this thing isn't over until that magic number is at zero. We have to keep our focus."

5. The Glavine-Smoltz duo guaranteed a lot of Braves success. As Tom said, "There's nothing better than a team that comes out of nowhere and finds themselves in the World Series."

6. Another great Atlanta hurler, Greg Maddux, summed up

pitching: "The best pitchers have a short-term memory and a bulletproof confidence."

7. Even perfectionist Maddux admitted he sometimes lapsed a bit: "I daydream just like everybody else. I just do it with my body facing the field, so everybody thinks I'm paying attention."

8. Dusty Baker was on deck for Atlanta when Aaron hit his record-breaking home run: "Everybody's the next somebody. I was the next Hank Aaron. You see what happened."

9. Baker admitted that, because he was from California, being drafted by Atlanta wasn't his first choice: "I didn't want to go to the South. There was a lot of racial unrest, riots, and freedom marches. There was nonconformity to everything. Vietnam. Racial issues."

10. In the end, Dusty was thankful for his luck: "I met a lot of good people, white and black. And I got to know Hank Aaron. Before I signed, he promised my mom he'd take care of me as if I was his own son. I was always with Hank. That's an experience I wouldn't trade for anything, and that's why I know God put me in a situation for a purpose."

CHAPTER 4:

BRAVE RECORDS

QUIZ TIME!

1. The Braves have retired numbers for 10 players and managers, besides the ubiquitous Jackie Robinson. Which of the following has NOT had his number retired?

   a. Bobby Cox
   b. Andruw Jones
   c. Chipper Jones
   d. Dale Murphy

2. No doubt, Hank Aaron holds almost every Braves batting record. In his 3,076 games played for the franchise, how many hits did he amass?

   a. 3,100
   b. 3,300
   c. 3,600
   d. 3,800

3. Surprisingly, a former player besides Aaron has the best Braves BA. Who is he?

a. Hugh Duffy
b. Rico Carty
c. Billy Hamilton
d. Chick Stahl

4. Which Braves speedster has the most career triples?

   a. Bill Bruton
   b. Herman Long
   c. Rabbit Maranville
   d. Sam Wise

5. In addition to playing in three different cities, how many different names has the team had over the years?

   a. 4
   b. 6
   c. 8
   d. 10

6. Amazingly, in 144 years and some 21,377 games in their illustrious history, the Braves barely squeak by with a winning record. What's their percentage?

   a. .501
   b. .505
   c. .512
   d. .525

7. In 1993, the Braves posted their best-ever average attendance per game in Atlanta-Fulton County Stadium. What was that average attendance?

   a. 43,420
   b. 45,880

c. 47,960

d. 49,555

8. In 25 playoff appearances, how many times have the Braves won the pennant?

a. 13

b. 15

c. 17

d. 19

9. In 1993, Atlanta also tipped the scales with more than 3.8 million fans on the season. Which of the following teams did NOT best that mark?

a. Cleveland

b. Colorado

c. New York Yankees

d. Toronto

10. In 2005, the Braves won their division yet again, completing a streak of 14 consecutive years, an MLB record.

a. True

b. False

11. That very same year, the "Baby Braves" had more than four rookies with more than 100 at-bats each, another MLB mark. Which of the following rookies did NOT have 100 at-bats?

a. Wilson Betemit

b. Kyle Davies

c. Brian McCann

d. Pete Orr

12. Despite a slow start in 2006, the Braves' bats came alive after the break. Chipper Jones tied an MLB record by hitting for extra bases in 14 straight games. Who had held that record for 69 years?

a. Steve Garvey
b. Hideki Matsui
c. Willie Stargell
d. Paul Waner

13. The first of three World Series wins by the Braves came in 1914 while still in Boston. Who was the manager at the time?

a. Fred Haney
b. Russ Nixon
c. George Stallings
d. Bobby Wine

14. A Brave for six years, which pitcher holds the record for fewest pitches (58) by one pitcher in a complete game?

a. Red Barrett
b. Jim Johnson
c. Kid Nichols
d. Mark Wohlers

15. In 1889, John Clarkson could do no wrong on the mound. What was the record he set for wins in a single season?

a. 35
b. 41
c. 49
d. 53

16. Speedster Otis Nixon nabbed a record number of stolen bases in a single Braves game. How many?

    a. 4
    b. 5
    c. 6
    d. 7

17. Of all the Braves with their numbers retired, only one was NOT elected to the Hall of Fame. Who was it?

    a. Tom Glavine
    b. Dale Murphy
    c. Phil Niekro
    d. John Smoltz

18. The first Dominican to play regularly in MLB, Felipe Alou was also a three-time All-Star and was elected to the Canadian and Caribbean Halls of Fame. How many times in his career did he lead off games with homers?

    a. 17
    b. 20
    c. 23
    d. 26

19. Which of the following Braves did NOT connect for four homers in a single game to tie the franchise record?

    a. Hank Aaron
    b. Joe Adcock
    c. Bob Horner
    d. Bobby Lowe

20. Phil Niekro's knuckler could literally get out of hand: He had 200 wild pitches in his Braves career. Who is second with 162?

   a. Tony Cloninger
   b. Kid Nichols
   c. Al Spalding
   d. Jim Whitney

QUIZ ANSWERS

1. B – Andruw Jones

2. C – 3,600

3. C – Billy Hamilton (.339)

4. C – Rabbit Maranville (103)

5. C – 8

6. A – .501

7. C – 47,960

8. C – 17

9. A – Cleveland

10. A – True

11. B – Kyle Davies

12. D – Paul Waner

13. C – George Stallings

14. A – Red Barrett

15. C – 49

16. C – 6

17. B – Dale Murphy

18. B – 20

19. A – Hank Aaron

20. D – Jim Whitney

DID YOU KNOW?

1. After winning the award with the Cubs in 1992, Greg Maddux then reeled off three straight Cy Young campaigns for Atlanta.

2. In 1999, MLB began handing out the Warren Spahn Award for the best left-handed pitcher in baseball.

3. Besides Hall-of-Famer Dennis Eckersley, John Smoltz is the only pitcher in MLB history with 150 wins and 150 saves.

4. Few MLB pitchers have played into their 50s (with Satchell Paige finally bowing out at 59). Phil Niekro was close, hanging up the spikes at 48 years and 179 days.

5. No superlatives can describe "Old Hoss" Radbourn's 1884 season with the Providence Grays (before he became a Brave): 60 wins, 1 save, and every inning pitched in three World Series wins.

6. The 1938 Braves were on the losing end of Johnny Vander Meer's no-hitter. He pitched another no-hitter four nights later to blank Brooklyn in the first-ever night game at Ebbets Field.

7. Even the History Channel commemorates the day Hank Aaron broke Babe Ruth's career home run record of 714 round-trippers: April 8, 1974, in front of 53,775 delirious Braves fans.

8. The fact that African-American Aaron received death threats and racist hate mail made the record seem bittersweet to many, including Aaron himself.

9. Yet another record Aaron broke was when he became one of the first African-American executives in MLB and a vocal proponent of minority hiring with the Atlanta franchise.

10. It's not a record, but maybe it should be: SunTrust (now Truist) Park has 11,000 parking spaces for its 42,000 seats.

CHAPTER 5:

HOW ABOUT A TRADE?

QUIZ TIME!

1. In 2008, the Braves unloaded Mark Teixeira to the Angels for relief pitchers Stephen Marek (who soon got hurt) and a light-hitting first baseman who was traded again after a mediocre year. Who was that first baseman?

   a. Omar Infante
   b. Kelly Johnson
   c. Casey Kotchman
   d. Brent Lillibridge

2. In 2015, the Braves acquired Zachary Bird and Hector Oliveira from the Dodgers for Bronson Arroyo and others. Oliveira played in 30 games and was then arrested, effectively ending his career. What was the charge?

   a. Armed robbery
   b. Domestic violence
   c. Drunk driving
   d. Jaywalking

3. The Braves gave up Doyle Alexander in 1987 for a Double-A pitcher who went on to become one of the franchise's greatest pitchers ever. Who?

   a. Tom Glavine
   b. Greg Maddux
   c. John Smoltz
   d. Jonny Venters

4. Fred McGriff got off to a "fiery" start with the Braves after his 1993 trade from San Diego: The press box caught fire on his first day. What was Fred's nickname?

   a. "The Crime Dog"
   b. "Fred Flintstone"
   c. "McGriff the Magic Man"
   d. "Massive McGriff"

5. In 1997, Atlanta traded two stars, David Justice and Marquis Grissom, for two others, including one who would last only a year before playing for 10 other clubs. Who was he?

   a. Jeff Blauser
   b. Andrés Galarraga
   c. Kenny Lofton
   d. Terry Pendleton

6. A's general manager Billy Beane gambled on Dan Meyer while trading Tim Hudson to the Braves. How many wins did Huddy pile up in Atlanta?

   a. 78
   b. 97

c. 113

d. 127

7. Which key player did the Braves trade away at the beginning of their huge rebuilding effort in 2014?

a. Todd Cunningham

b. Jason Heyward

c. B.J. Upton

d. Kyle Wren

8. In exchange for Heyward, the Braves picked up pitcher Shelby Miller, who racked up 33 starts and a 3.02 ERA in 2014. Where did he come from?

a. Arizona

b. Houston

c. Philadelphia

d. St. Louis

9. Why was Rogers Hornsby, one of MLB's greatest hitters ever, traded by the New York Giants to the Boston Braves in 1928?

a. Alcohol problems

b. Gambling problems at the race track

c. Gambling problems in casinos

d. Womanizing

10. After only a year in Boston, again as the league's best hitter, the Cubs offered five players and a bundle of money for Hornsby to help the cash-strapped Braves. How much?

a. $75,000

b. $125,000

c. $200,000

d. $350,000

11. In late 2015, Atlanta gave up two pitchers for Dansby Swanson who turned himself into a starting shortstop. Which other Gold Glove winner came along?

a. Johan Camargo

b. Ender Inciarte

c. Rio Ruiz

d. Drew Stubbs

12. The Braves swapped a pitcher to the Cards in 2003 who contributed to the Red Birds' staff for almost a decade. Who was the righty?

a. Jung Bong

b. Will Cunnane

c. Joey Dawley

d. Adam Wainwright

13. When John Schuerholz traded Mark Teixeira just before the 2008 trade deadline, what did Atlanta get?

a. "A minimal return"

b. Five players "to be named later"

c. Nothing

d. Two compensatory draft picks in 2009

14. The Braves acquired Royal Michael Tucker in 1997 and traded him away two years later for Boone and Remlinger.

That helped Atlanta make the World Series how many times in nine years?

a. 2

b. 4

c. 5

d. 7

15. In 1914, Braves manager George Stallings introduced "platooning" to his team as he traded for a light-hitting Card named after an animal. Who was it?

a. Johnny "Antelope" Evers

b. Rabbit Maranville

c. Hub "Panther" Perdue

d. Possum Whitted

16. "Red" Smith became a Brave in 1914, traded after a fight with his Brooklyn Robins manager. What did he do for the city of Atlanta after his baseball career?

a. Repo man

b. Sanitary engineer

c. Schoolteacher

d. Tax investigator

17. What was one reason given for the St. Louis Browns trading Jeff Heath to the Braves for cash considerations in 1948?

a. His "devil part"

b. His inability to run

c. His non-existent arm

d. His weak bat

18. In 1957, the Braves traded for a veteran "redhead" who made everyone feel like "Superman," had a hot bat, and became the team leader. What was his name?

    a. Ray Schadiest
    b. Ray Schaeffer
    c. Red Schoendienst
    d. Red Schooner

19. The Chicago Cubs' infield trio became part of a 1910 poem that said: "These are the saddest of possible words, 'Tinker to Evers to Chance.'" Which one wound up with the Braves?

    a. Frank Chance
    b. Johnny Evers
    c. Joe Tinker

20. Which of the following was NOT a reason for many to doubt Johnny's ability to contribute to the Braves?

    a. His age (32)
    b. His height (5'9")
    c. His pigeon toes
    d. His tendency to get ejected

QUIZ ANSWERS

1. C – Casey Kotchman

2. B – Domestic violence

3. C – John Smoltz

4. A – "The Crime Dog"

5. C – Kenny Lofton

6. C – 113

7. B – Jason Heyward

8. D – St. Louis

9. B – Gambling problems at the race track

10. C – $200,000 (almost $3 million today)

11. B – Ender Inciarte

12. D – Adam Wainwright

13. A – "A minimal return"

14. C – 5

15. D – Possum Whitted

16. D – Tax investigator

17. A – His "devil part"

18. C – Red Schoendienst

19. B – Johnny Evers

20. C – His pigeon toes

DID YOU KNOW?

1. John Smoltz also holds the distinction of being the only Brave on the 40-man roster to have participated in all 14 straight division titles.

2. When Jeff Heath asked his manager for a day off near the end of the season to rest in order to kick his former team's tail, he was denied. The next game, he broke his leg sliding, missed the series, and the Braves lost the '48 World Series to Cleveland.

3. After the 1958 Series, doctors found that Red Schoendienst had tuberculosis. He had part of his lung removed, came back as a pinch-hitter, and made it to the Hall. "I never thought that milk truck ride (to St. Louis) would eventually lead to Cooperstown," he quipped.

4. In Maranville's book *Run Rabbit Run*, the infielder said he was amazed by Johnny's feel for the game: "Evers was psychic. He could sense where a player was going to hit if the pitcher threw the ball where he was supposed to."

5. In 2001, when assistant general manager Frank Wren "discovered" Julio Franco and brought him on board, they found out he was really 43 years old, not 40.

6. Franco knocked the cover off the ball, especially against future Hall-of-Famer Randy Johnson in Game 7 of the NLCS. Julio stayed a Brave until age 49.

7. John Schuerholz watched the Pirates' Denny Neagle handle the Braves on August 27, 1996, and then traded for him. The Braves already led the NL East by 11 games at the time.

8. Braves manager Billy Southworth engineered the 1946 deal for Pittsburgh's Bob Elliott. Billy told Bob, "If you hustle, I'm absolutely convinced that you will win the MVP Award this season." Bob did just that.

9. Johnny Sain dominated on the mound but made a mere $25,000 with the Braves from 1946 to 1951. He later returned as Atlanta's pitching coach and mentored coaching legend Leo Mazzone.

10. When the Braves signed Dick "Baldy" Rudolph for $5,000 in 1913, he was on the verge of quitting. He soon shut down the Philadelphia A's and their ace, "Chief" Bender, in the Series.

CHAPTER 6:

CHAT ABOUT STATS

QUIZ TIME!

1. Bobby Cox is the winningest Braves manager. What was his percentage as skipper?

   a. .501

   b. .525

   c. .557

   d. .569

2. Considered one of the best Braves in recent memory, what was first baseman Freddy Freeman's salary in 2019?

   a. $10 million

   b. $16 million

   c. $21 million

   d. $24 million

3. That same year, the Braves fell to the Cards at home to lose the NLDS, 3-2. How many runs did St. Louis score in the first inning of the last game to walk away?

   a. 5

   b. 8

c. 10

d. 13

4. When the Braves clinched the 1995 Series over Cleveland, they became the first club to win the Fall Classic in three separate cities.

   a. True

   b. False

5. That Series was also noteworthy because five of the six games were won by a single run. What other pitcher helped Tom Glavine win Game 6 on a combined one-hitter?

   a. Brad Clontz

   b. Pedro Borbón

   c. Kent Mercker

   d. Mark Wohlers

6. Opening Day starter Greg Maddux won his sixth straight Gold Glove Award in 1995. How many did he win during his career?

   a. 8

   b. 10

   c. 13

   d. 15

7. Before 1995, the Braves last won the Series in 1957, battering the Yankees (4-3). What was the name of their Milwaukee ballpark at the time?

   a. Borchert Field

   b. County Stadium

c. Miller Park

d. Milwaukee Baseball Grounds

8. Using the "Pythagorean W-L" stat, the '57 Braves racked up a lot more runs than they yielded. How many, to be exact?

a. 736/642

b. 751/633

c. 772/613

d. 798/600

9. On that bat-happy 1957 squad, who was the only player who got into seven games but managed a .000 batting average?

a. Nippy Jones

b. Del Rice

c. Chuck Tanner

d. Hawk Taylor

10. Of the four starting pitchers on that 1957 Braves team, who was the only one who didn't have a winning record?

a. Bob Buhl

b. Lew Burdette

c. Gene Conley

d. Warren Spahn

11. Truist Park opened on April 13, 2017. What was its cost?

a. $550 million

b. $628 million

c. $666 million

d. $672 million

12. The stadium was originally named SunTrust Park, but renamed Truist in early 2020 after a corporate merger. With whom?

    a. AT&T
    b. BB&T
    c. Home Depot
    d. Newell Rubbermaid

13. What is the name of the large kid-friendly area behind the left-field grandstand?

    a. Chop House
    b. Delta Sky360 Club
    c. Hope & Will's Sandlot
    d. Terrace Club

14. The 2017 opening of the new park saw the Braves record a big win against which opponent?

    a. Astros
    b. Giants
    c. Mets
    d. Padres

15. Replacing Homer the Brave, the new Braves mascot was "blasted" on social media upon arrival in 2018. What is its name?

    a. Blooper
    b. Luchador
    c. Screech
    d. Wally

16. In his career, Greg Maddux faced 20,421 batters. How many of them faced a 3-0 count?

    a. 91
    b. 133
    c. 344
    d. 587

17. Maddux allowed as many home runs in his first five seasons with the Braves (1,156 innings) as _____ did in 2011.

    a. Bronson Arroyo
    b. Josh Beckett
    c. Clayton Kershaw
    d. Justin Verlander

18. On July 26, 2011, the Braves secured a walk-off 4-3 victory against the Pirates. How many innings did the game go?

    a. 13
    b. 15
    c. 17
    d. 19

19. Even though Warren Spahn never had more than 200 strikeouts in a season, how many campaigns of 200+ innings did he record in succession?

    a. 11
    b. 14
    c. 17
    d. 21

20. John Smoltz did it all for the Braves, as both a starting pitcher and reliever. What percentage of votes did he receive on his Hall of Fame ballot in 2015?

   a. 79.9
   b. 82.9
   c. 85.6
   d. 88.4

QUIZ ANSWERS

1. C – .557

2. C – $21 million

3. C – 10 (Cards won, 13-1)

4. A – True

5. D – Mark Wohlers

6. C – 13

7. B – County Stadium

8. C – 772/613

9. D – Hawk Taylor

10. C – Gene Conley (9 W, 9 L)

11. D – $672 million

12. B – BB&T (Truist Financial)

13. C – Hope & Will's Sandlot

14. D – Padres

15. A – Blooper

16. B – 133

17. A – Bronson Arroyo

18. D – 19

19. C – 17

20. B – 82.9

DID YOU KNOW?

1. Spahn pitched 208 complete games between the ages of 30 and 39. "A pitcher needs two pitches—one they're looking for, and one to cross them up," he quipped.

2. John Smoltz pitched for Atlanta over a 12-year span as a starter, giving up a stingy 2.9 free passes per nine innings.

3. Chipper Jones hauled in every kind of award only as a Brave for 19 seasons, including the last of his eight All-Star nominations at age 40.

4. Including his MVP trophy in 1999 and Rookie of the Year runner-up in 1995, Chipper finished in the top 10 for MVP consideration in five other years.

5. Jones ranks in the top 10 of all third basemen in MLB history in 10 different statistical categories.

6. Eddie Mathews also played the hot corner for the Braves in three different cities, never hitting fewer than 23 homers per year from his rookie campaign in 1952 until 1966.

7. Ronald Acuña Jr. fell one shy of the prestigious "40-40 Club" in 2019 when he belted 41 homers and stole 37 bases. At 21, he was the youngest player in history to go 35-35.

8. At 21 years and 215 days old, Acuña became the fourth-youngest player to hit 50 home runs in his brief career, trailing only Mel Ott (20 years, 166 days), Tony Conigliaro, and Andruw Jones.

9. On June 27, 1998, Maddux shut down Toronto in his fastest complete game: one hour and 46 minutes. He notched 13 strikeouts.

10. Panamanian Johan Camargo played for the Carolina Mudcats, Gwinnett Stripers, and Florida Fire Frogs before batting .233 for the Braves in 2019.

CHAPTER 7:

DRAFT DAY

QUIZ TIME!

1. Since the draft was established in 1965, how many players have the Braves chosen during the 1st round?

    a. 42

    b. 50

    c. 56

    d. 66

2. Which state leads the Atlanta parade of draftees over the years?

    a. California

    b. Florida

    c. Georgia

    d. Texas

3. Which of the following members of the 1995 championship team was NOT a draft pick?

    a. Steve Avery

    b. Chipper Jones

   c. Kent Mercker

   d. Jason Schmidt

4. When the Braves twice owned the 1ˢᵗ overall pick (in 1978 and 1990), which player did they NOT select?

   a. Bob Horner

   b. Chipper Jones

   c. Rusty Richards

5. Only two of Atlanta's selections have come from outside the USA. Where was Scott Thorman drafted from in 2000?

   a. Ontario, Canada

   b. Amsterdam, Holland

   c. San Juan, Puerto Rico

   d. Seoul, South Korea

6. When the Braves were unable to sign 1995 pick Chad Hutchinson, whom did they select as a compensatory pick in 1996?

   a. Joe Ayrault

   b. Jermaine Dye

   c. Tony Graffanino

   d. Jason Marquis

7. In 1965, the first year of the modern draft, Atlanta picked first baseman Dick Grant. What was his hometown?

   a. Sacramento, California

   b. Pensacola, Florida

   c. Watertown, Massachusetts

   d. Palmyra, Pennsylvania

8. Dale Murphy, drafted in 1974, won numerous awards as a Brave. Which of these was NOT one of them?

   a. Hank Aaron Hitter's Award
   b. Lou Gehrig Memorial Award
   c. NL MVP
   d. Roberto Clemente Award

9. A local outfielder from Lilburn, drafted in 2002, won a Gold Glove Award in 2007. Who was he?

   a. Jeff Francoeur
   b. Johnny Mize
   c. Tony Phillips
   d. Cecil Travis

10. When Atlanta signed free agent B.J. Upton in 2013, they lost their original 1st round pick. To which team?

    a. Detroit
    b. Miami
    c. Tampa Bay
    d. San Diego

11. Pundits consider the 2004 Draft a bust for the Braves as only two of their top picks made it to the Major Leagues. How many top picks did they have?

    a. 9
    b. 13
    c. 17
    d. 24

12. Joey Devine, Atlanta's top pick in 2005, had the dubious distinction of standing on the mound as the Braves fell to the Astros in 18 innings in the first round's final game. What happened?

   a. He allowed a run-scoring double.
   b. He balked in the winning run.
   c. He gave up a walk-off homer.
   d. He walked in the winning run.

13. Yunel Escobar was considered the prime find in the 2005 Draft. Where did he come from?

   a. Cuba
   b. Dominican Republic
   c. Upstate New York
   d. Venezuela

14. The Braves opted for free-swinging Cody Johnson in the 2006 Draft. How many strikeouts did he rack up in 127 games in 2008?

   a. 127
   b. 145
   c. 165
   d. 177

15. In 2009, the Braves' top pick was pitcher Mike Minor, but they could have drafted a player with a "higher ceiling." What does that mean?

   a. Higher number of Instagram followers
   b. Higher potential

c. Higher salary

d. Higher stats

16. Which Braves pitcher was drafted with the 29th pick in 2000, never played for Atlanta, and was part of "the trade no Braves fan likes to talk about"?

    a. Aaron Herr

    b. Tripper Johnson

    c. Macay McBride

    d. Adam Wainwright

17. The Braves got their man Bob Horner in the 1978 Draft. Which other team had already selected Horner in 1975?

    a. Arizona

    b. Milwaukee

    c. Oakland

    d. Pittsburgh

18. Jason Heyward went to high school in Atlanta and was the Braves' top pick in 2007. What's the power hitter's nickname?

    a. "Hey-J"

    b. "J-Hey"

    c. "Jason the Hit Man"

    d. "Jaseward"

19. Steve Avery was the 3rd overall pick in 1988. Atlanta's "Young Guns" included Avery, Glavine, and Smoltz. Who was the group's fourth pitcher?

    a. José Álvarez

    b. German Jimenez

c. Pete Smith

d. Bruce Sutter

20. Ian Anderson was picked 3rd overall by the Braves in 2016. What is his current ranking in the list of "best baseball prospects" on MLB.com?

   a. 15th

   b. 24th

   c. 37th

   d. 52nd

QUIZ ANSWERS

1. C – 56

2. B – Florida

3. D – Jason Schmidt

4. C – Rusty Richards

5. A – Ontario, Canada

6. D – Jason Marquis

7. C – Watertown, Massachusetts

8. A – Hank Aaron Hitter's Award

9. A – Jeff Francoeur

10. C – Tampa Bay

11. C – 17

12. C – He gave up a walk-off homer.

13. A – Cuba

14. D – 177

15. B – Higher potential

16. D – Adam Wainwright

17. C – Oakland

18. B – "J-Hey"

19. C – Pete Smith

20. C – 37th

DID YOU KNOW?

1. Drafted 3rd overall by the Braves in 1988, Avery came to the rescue in Atlanta's worst-to-first season of 1991. His 5.2 WAR (wins above replacement) was the best of his career.

2. Not long after Heyward was drafted, Bobby Cox compared the sound of the ball off Jason's bat to that of Mickey Mantle and even Hammerin' Hank.

3. Heyward was traded to the Cards in 2015. Besides his hitting prowess, he led outfielders in most defensive runs saved since 2010.

4. Even though Atlanta got J.D. Drew and Eli Marrero for top pick Adam Wainwright, fans still lamented the trade, especially since Adam closed out the 2006 Series against the Tigers for his new Cards team.

5. Bob Horner bashed all kinds of records at Arizona State (career homers, single-season dingers, and College World Series MVP), all leading to his 1st round selection by Atlanta in 1978.

6. Horner is one of only a few players to go straight from college to MLB starter without a day in the Minors. He homered in his first Braves game off future Famer Bert Blyleven.

7. Drafted by Atlanta in 1974, Dale Murphy successfully shifted from catcher to the outfield. In 1982, Murph won the first MVP for a Brave since Aaron in 1957.

8. After his selection, Dale became the International League Rookie of the Year with the Richmond Braves. But 1982 was his year in Atlanta, when he won the MVP and became the third Brave ever to appear in all 162 games.

9. Larry Wayne "Chipper" Jones Jr. was the first Atlanta pick and the first selection of the entire 1990 Draft. He quickly turned into Atlanta's primary third baseman where he stayed till 2012.

10. One of the reasons Atlanta picked Chipper was that highly touted pitcher Todd Van Poppel claimed he would rather play for the Texas Longhorns than the "lowly" Braves.

CHAPTER 8:

PITCHER & CATCHER TIDBITS

QUIZ TIME!

1. The 1991 Braves team started a streak of NL success. How many wins did Tom Glavine and Steve Avery combine for on the mound?

   a. 30

   b. 34

   c. 38

   d. 46

2. When the Braves finally fell to the Twins in the tenth inning of Game 7 of the 1991 Series, it was called one of the greatest pitching duels ever. Who was John Smoltz's opponent?

   a. Allan Anderson

   b. Scott Erickson

   c. Jack Morris

   d. Kevin Tapani

3. Atlanta's 1997 pitching staff is sometimes called the best in Braves history. Who led the team with 20 wins?

    a. Tom Glavine
    b. Greg Maddux
    c. Denny Neagle
    d. John Smoltz

4. In 2003, Smoltz was smoking, racking up a record number of saves before the All-Star break. How many?

    a. 22
    b. 28
    c. 34
    d. 40

5. Among the catchers handling the 2003 staff, Javy López put up big offensive numbers. How many RBI did he have?

    a. 89
    b. 99
    c. 109
    d. 119

6. That season, López broke the record for homers in a season by a catcher with 43. Who held the previous record of 41?

    a. Johnny Bench
    b. Todd Hundley
    c. Thurman Munson
    d. Iván Rodríguez

7. Which special event did Javy participate in on April 8, 1994?

    a. He caught Kent Mercker's no-hitter.

    b. He caught Tom Glavine's perfect game.

    c. He caught two no-hitters in a doubleheader.

    d. He entertained friends at his 24th birthday party.

8. Braves hurler Tom Glavine was named World Series MVP in 1995. How many Cleveland runs did he allow in his two games?

    a. 0

    b. 2

    c. 3

    d. 4

9. A few weeks into the 1961 campaign, the Braves had to call on rookie Joe Torre to grab the catcher's mitt. Which injured backstop did he replace?

    a. Yogi Berra

    b. Smoky Burgess

    c. Del Crandall

    d. Dutch Dotterer

10. Torre later led a certain team to victory over the Braves in both the 1996 and 1999 World Series. Which team?

    a. Brewers

    b. Indians

    c. Tigers

    d. Yankees

11. When considering a stat called "weighted runs created plus" that accounts for external factors like ballparks and eras, which Braves catcher stands on top?

    a. Javy López
    b. Brian McCann
    c. Eddie Pérez
    d. Joe Torre

12. While catching for Atlanta from 2005 to 2013, Brian McCann's WAR number ranks behind only one other backstop. Who?

    a. Jonathan Lucroy
    b. Joe Mauer
    c. Yadier Molina
    d. Buster Posey

13. Starting in the late 1940s, Del Crandall was behind the plate for Lew Burdette's brilliant game in the 1957 Series. At what age did Del first grace the Braves' lineup?

    a. 17
    b. 18
    c. 19
    d. 21

14. Even though Eddie Pérez was primarily a backup, he caught more Maddux innings than any other Brave. How many more?

    a. 188
    b. 218

c. 248

d. 309

15. When the Braves made their unbelievable Series run in 1991, who was mainly behind the plate?

   a. Bruce Benedict
   b. Ron Hassey
   c. Greg Olson
   d. Junior Ortiz

16. Benedict "Biff" Pocoroba was forced to give up his Braves catching duties in 1984 after injuries cut into his playing time. What Atlanta business did he then start?

   a. Selling carpets
   b. Selling insurance
   c. Selling sausages
   d. Selling used cars

17. The 1948 poem, "Spahn and Sain, then pray for rain," was inspired by the two Braves pitchers' unbridled success. In one 12-game span that year, what was their combined record?

   a. 12-0
   b. 11-1
   c. 10-2
   d. 9-3

18. Sain was brilliant and controversial, both as a player and later as a coach. He often ignored running drills, despised by pitchers. What was his quote on running?

a. "You don't pitch running."

b. "You don't run the damn ball across the plate."

c. "Running doesn't do much for your arm."

d. "If I wanted to run, I'd have joined a track team."

19. Spahn said, "Hitting is timing. Pitching is upsetting timing." What phrase was used to describe Warren?

a. "A cerebral workhorse"

b. "A mental mound dweller"

c. "A thinking man's pitcher"

d. "A thought-provoking player"

20. If Spahn had managed one more career win, who would he have tied for fifth on MLB's all-time list?

a. Pud Galvin

b. Walter Johnson

c. Christy Mathewson

d. Cy Young

QUIZ ANSWERS

1. C – 38

2. C – Jack Morris

3. C – Denny Neagle

4. C – 34

5. C – 109

6. B – Todd Hundley

7. A – He caught Kent Mercker's no-hitter.

8. B – 2

9. C – Del Crandall

10. D – Yankees

11. D – Joe Torre

12. B – Joe Mauer

13. C – 19

14. C – 248

15. C – Greg Olson

16. C – Selling sausages

17. A – 12-0

18. B – "You don't run the ball across the damn plate."

19. C – "A thinking man's pitcher"

20. A – Pud Galvin

DID YOU KNOW?

1. Johnny Sain had the distinction of being the first pitcher to face Jackie Robinson in the Majors (1946) and the last to pitch against the Babe (in a 1943 Red Cross exhibition game).

2. Out of Broken Arrow, Oklahoma, Warren Spahn holds the MLB record for most career wins by a left-hander, all after the live-ball era began in 1920. He had 13 seasons with 20 or more wins.

3. Since 1920, among pitchers with at least 3,000 innings under their belts, 1957 Braves ace Lew Burdette trails only four pitchers (including Greg Maddux) in walks per nine innings (1.84).

4. Milwaukee won the 1957 Series behind Burdette. Blanking the Yanks twice, he hurled three complete-game wins— the first time any pitcher had done so since Christy Mathewson in 1905.

5. Considering that Phil Niekro was an All-Star five times and pitched for the Braves for 20 years, the $250 that Milwaukee paid for him in 1959 seems like a good investment.

6. In 1982, at age 43, "Knucksie" Niekro beat the Padres almost single-handedly, tossing a complete-game shutout and clouting a two-run homer.

7. If his pitching wasn't good enough, Greg Maddux was MLB's best fielding pitcher. With lightning reflexes, he won a Gold Glove every year in Atlanta except one.

8. Tom Glavine was drafted by both the Braves and hockey's Los Angeles Kings. He went 7-17 in his first full year (1988), but stayed away from the puck, won 20 games in 1991, and took Atlanta to the World Series for the first time in 33 years.

9. Glavine pitched decisively in Game 6 of the 1995 Series to beat Cleveland. It took some heat off Tom, a notable union rep who was booed by home fans after the dismal work stoppage.

10. When John Smoltz bounced back from arm surgery in 2001, he moved smoothly into the closer role and racked up an NL-record 55 saves.

CHAPTER 9:

ODDS & ENDS

QUIZ TIME!

1. How many rookies did the Braves have on their 2005 roster?

   a. 9
   b. 12
   c. 15
   d. 18

2. Which Brave became the youngest player ever to hit a home run in the World Series?

   a. Hank Aaron
   b. Ronald Acuña Jr.
   c. Wes Covington
   d. Andruw Jones

3. During their 13 years in Milwaukee, how many losing campaigns did the Braves have?

   a. 0
   b. 4

c. 6

d. 8

4. When Rabbit Maranville finally hung up his spikes in 1935, he had played 23 seasons in the NL. That record was finally broken in 1986. By whom?

   a. Rickey Henderson

   b. Tommy John

   c. Cal Ripken

   d. Pete Rose

5. On August 10, 1944, Red Barrett shut down the Reds in the "most efficient game" ever. How many pitches did he need in the 2-0 win?

   a. 48

   b. 58

   c. 65

   d. 72

6. Which of the Braves' farm teams is located farthest west?

   a. Danville (Virginia) Braves

   b. Florida Fire Frogs

   c. Mississippi Braves

   d. Rome (Georgia) Braves

7. Atlanta Stadium opened in 1965 with the Milwaukee Braves visiting for a three-game exhibition against Detroit. Which team occupied the stadium until the Braves moved for good in 1966?

   a. Atlanta Crackers

   b. Atlanta Dream

c. Atlanta Falcons

d. Georgia Swarm

8. Which player became the first Atlanta Brave ever to engineer an unassisted triple play?

a. Josh Donaldson

b. Rafael Furcal

c. Herman Long

d. Félix "The Kitten" Millán

9. One Braves slugger liked "Here I Go" by Mystikal as his intro music. His wife, gospel singer DeLeon, also sang the national anthem at a 1999 Dodgers game. Who was he?

a. Andrés Galarraga

b. Brian Jordan

c. Ryan Klesko

d. Gary Sheffield

10. What was the street address of the old Turner Field?

a. 755 Battery Avenue SE

b. 715 Hank Aaron Drive

c. 755 Hank Aaron Drive

d. 190 Marietta Street NW

11. In the 1980s, cheers for the Braves were led by a man in a monk's outfit atop the dugout. How was he referred to?

a. Brother Bob

b. Brother Francis

c. The Brave Friar

d. The Mad Monk

12. Before winning as the Braves' skipper in 1995, Bobby Cox also helped the Yankees capture the 1977 World Series. What was his job there?

    a. First-base coach
    b. Manager
    c. Pitching coach
    d. Third-base coach

13. Tony Cloninger showed his great arm with 24 wins in Milwaukee in 1965. The move to Atlanta helped his hitting with two grand slams in one game and nine RBI in another in 1966.

    a. True
    b. False

14. The man who launched the ceremonial first pitch for the Braves' first game in Atlanta was an outspoken Civil Rights advocate who helped bring pro sports to Atlanta. Who was he?

    a. Mayor Ivan Allen Jr.
    b. Howard Callaway
    c. Lester Maddox
    d. Chris Tucker

15. The Braves drafted Randy Johnson in 1982, but he decided he wanted to go to college rather than play in Atlanta. He went on to star for the Mariners and Diamondbacks. What college grabbed him?

    a. Pepperdine
    b. Seattle Pacific University

c. UCLA

d. USC

16. Félix Mantilla roomed with Hank Aaron before they got their big-league break with the Braves. In what minor-league city were they roomies?

a. Jacksonville, Florida

b. Macon, Georgia

c. Pearl, Mississippi

d. Richmond, Virginia

17. To which Braves manager is the following quote attributed: "Good pitching will always stop good hitting, and vice versa."?

a. Bobby Cox

b. Brian Snitker

c. Casey Stengel

d. Bobby Wine

18. John Rocker became nationally known for his running charge out of the Braves' bullpen. What was the apparent reason he was traded to Cleveland?

a. Insubordination

b. Racism

c. Sexual harassment

d. Wildness

19. In the 1980s, Chief Noc-A-Homa emerged from his teepee to dance when a Brave clubbed a homer. Which indigenous tribe did he belong to?

a. Cherokee (Oklahoma)

b. Iroquois (New York)

c. Odawa (Ontario)

d. Seminole (Florida)

20. Which Padres player (who also played for the Braves) made the last out in Phil Niekro's no-hitter on August 5, 1973?

a. Cito Gaston

b. Johnny Grubb

c. Leron Lee

d. Gene Locklear

QUIZ ANSWERS

1. D – 18

2. D – Andruw Jones (19 years, 180 days)

3. A – 0

4. D – Pete Rose

5. B – 58

6. C – Mississippi Braves

7. A – Atlanta Crackers

8. B – Rafael Furcal

9. D – Gary Sheffield

10. C – 755 Hank Aaron Drive

11. B – Brother Francis

12. A – First-base coach

13. A – True

14. A – Mayor Ivan Allen Jr.

15. D – USC

16. A – Jacksonville, Florida

17. C – Casey Stengel (1938-1943)

18. B – Racism

19. C – Odawa (Ontario) (Levi Walker Jr. was the Chief.)

20. A – Cito Gaston

DID YOU KNOW?

1. David Justice was the 1990 NL Rookie of the Year after beloved Dale Murphy was traded to the Phils. David criticized Atlanta's fans for lack of support, but he hit the home run that clinched the 1995 World Series.

2. Milwaukee's County Stadium had a grove of trees behind it called "Perini's Woods" in honor of owner Lou Perini, who moved the team to the Midwest.

3. Tommie Aaron's 13 home runs didn't quite match his brother's output. But together they set the MLB record for most homers by a pair of brothers, besting Eddie Murray and sibling Rich.

4. Kid Nichols won 362 games in a career that began as a Boston Beaneater. He was proud of two things: His election to the Hall of Fame and the fact that he had never been replaced by a reliever.

5. Besides the Waffle House and the Terrapin Taproom, Truist Park features "the Best Darn Steak Sandwich in Baseball" at the Carvery.

6. If that delicacy doesn't satisfy you, then look for the "fried tomahawk pork chop" at Braves Big Bites, or perhaps the "blackened catfish po' boy taco" at the Taco Factory.

7. Ted Turner founded TV networks TBS and CNN, and World Championship Wrestling (WCW). He's the largest

private landowner in the USA (1.75 million acres), and he owned the Braves when they won the '95 Series.

8. In 1977, Atlanta sank into a slump. Turner sent manager Dave Bristol on a "scouting trip" and took over the team. Bounced in the next game by Pittsburgh, NL President Chub Feeney and Commissioner Bowie Kuhn ordered Turner out as manager.

9. The Caray family certainly added color to Braves broadcasts over the years. Dad Skip shared humor and "homerism" with Atlanta fans for 30 years before turning the reins over to son Chip.

10. Of all the records that Aaron set in his years with the Braves, he didn't set the strikeout mark. Hank whiffed 1,294 times in 21 seasons, while Dale Murphy fanned 1,581 times in 15.

CHAPTER 10:

WHO'S ON FIRST?

QUIZ TIME!

1. Joe Adcock played first for the big-swinging Milwaukee teams in the 1950s. He retired with the third-highest fielding percentage of any first baseman. What was it?

   a. .978
   b. .986
   c. .994
   d. .997

2. Born in Coushatta, Louisiana, Adcock attended Louisiana State University. Before college, he had never played in an organized baseball game in his life.

   a. True
   b. False

3. This first baseman was a Boston Beaneater in the late 1800s. He was credited with inventing the 3-6-3 double play, playing off the first base foul line and deep like fielders today. Who was he?

a. Bobby Lowe

b. Billy Nash

c. Fred Tenney

d. Tommy Tucker

4. Baxter "Buck" Jordan became the Braves' regular first baseman in 1933, and twice in his career he collected eight hits in a doubleheader. Where was he born?

   a. Blowing Rock, North Carolina

   b. Clemson, South Carolina

   c. Cooleemee, North Carolina

   d. Travelers Rest, South Carolina

5. Chris Chambliss played first for the Braves from 1980 to 1986. He had only one at-bat with the Yanks in 1988, struck out, and then retired. How much did that sole plate appearance earn him?

   a. $10,000

   b. $14,000

   c. $20,000

   d. $40,000

6. Bob Horner moved from third to first with the Braves due to injuries that hurt his mobility. Which Japanese team did he join for one year in 1987?

   a. Hiroshima Toyo Carp

   b. Hokkaido Nippon-Ham Fighters

   c. Yakult Swallows

   d. Yomiuri Giants

7. First baseman Fred McGriff's 493 career homers left him five short of "the 500 HR Club." Whom did he tie in the all-time ranking?

    a. Lou Gehrig
    b. Mickey Mantle
    c. Willie Mays
    d. Gary Sheffield

8. McGriff's nickname, "Crime Dog," created by announcer Chris Berman, came from a cartoon dog designed to help police teach kids crime prevention. What was the mutt's name?

    a. Fido
    b. McGruff
    c. Mike McLick
    d. McSafe

9. Dominican Julio Franco had two stints with the Braves, as well as a pair with the Chiba Lotte Marines in Japan. How many other teams did he play for?

    a. 5
    b. 7
    c. 9
    d. 11

10. Andrés Galarraga was called "The Big Cat" for his defensive skills at first. Which of the following awards did he NOT receive?

    a. Gold Glove
    b. MLB Comeback Player of the Year

c. MVP

d. Silver Slugger

11. Galarraga's first season in Atlanta quieted critics: the first player in MLB history to hit 40+ homers in consecutive seasons for different teams. How many homers did he end up with in 1998?

    a. 40

    b. 44

    c. 48

    d. 51

12. With both parents born in Canada, Braves first baseman Freddie Freeman holds dual citizenship. Which team did he support growing up?

    a. Chicago Cubs

    b. Los Angeles Angels

    c. Los Angeles Dodgers

    d. Montreal Expos

13. Starting at first for the Braves in 2011, Freeman finished second to a teammate in the Rookie of the Year vote. Who was the winner?

    a. Craig Kimbrel

    b. Antoan Richardson

    c. Dan Uggla

    d. Vance Worley

14. Back in Atlanta after Series success with the Nats, Matt "Big City" Adams holds records for batting average (.473)

and slugging percentage (.754) at his university. Which one is it?

a. Bucknell University
b. Penn State University
c. Slippery Rock University
d. University of Pittsburgh

15. Mark Teixeira was traded to the Braves in 2007 after turning down an eight-year contract extension with Texas. How much was the extension worth?

a. $80 million
b. $100 million
c. $120 million
d. $140 million

16. Teixeira became the second Brave to homer in his first three games with the team. Who was the first?

a. Hank Aaron
b. Andruw Jones
c. Gary Sheffield
d. Joe Torre

17. Sidney Eugene Bream saw limited time with Atlanta due to injuries but scored the winning run in the 1992 NLCS to send the Braves to the World Series. Who was the opponent?

a. New York Mets
b. Pittsburgh
c. Philadelphia
d. Toronto

18. Casey Kotchman came from Anaheim in 2008 in a trade for Mark Teixeira. What was Casey's batting average in his 20 Atlanta games?

    a. .145
    b. .157
    c. .170
    d. .188

19. Jarrod "Salty" Saltalamacchia set the record for the longest last name in MLB history at 14 characters. What's the translation from Italian?

    a. "Jump as high as you can shouting"
    b. "Jump over the thicket"
    c. "Leap over the canyon"
    d. "Light the fire slowly"

20. Derrek Lee was traded to the Braves and saw action at first in the 2010 NLDS. With which team did he win the World Series in 2003, snuffing out a Yanks rally with a great catch?

    a. Chicago Cubs
    b. Florida Marlins
    c. Pittsburgh Pirates
    d. San Diego Padres

QUIZ ANSWERS

1. C – .994

2. A – True

3. C – Fred Tenney

4. C – Cooleemee, North Carolina

5. C – $20,000 (minimum player salary at the time)

6. C – Yakult Swallows

7. A – Lou Gehrig

8. B – McGruff

9. C – 9

10. C – MVP

11. B – 44

12. B – Los Angeles Angels

13. A – Craig Kimbrel

14. C – Slippery Rock University

15. D – $140 million

16. C – Gary Sheffield

17. B – Pittsburgh

18. B – .157

19. B – "Jump over the thicket"

20. B – Florida Marlins

DID YOU KNOW?

1. Derrek Lee's father, Leon, and his uncle, Leron, both played pro in Japan. D-Lee spent his summers in the Far East in high school.

2. First baseman Eric Hinske has various nicknames: "Big Damage" and "Big Diesel" among them. His dramatic pinch-hit homer put Atlanta ahead of the Giants in Game 3 of the 2010 NLDS (San Francisco eventually won).

3. In 2008, Mark Kotsay became the first Atlanta player to hit for the cycle since Albert Hall in 1987. He even hit another single in the ninth, but the Braves lost to the Cubs, 11-7.

4. Unfortunately, Ryan Klesko's father passed away at an early age. His mother, Lorene, built a pitcher's mound for Ryan, and put on catcher's gear three times a week to help the youngster.

5. Klesko's three homers against the Indians helped the Braves capture the 1995 Series. His Game 5 blast in the ninth inning was almost caught by his mother.

6. In 1988, Gerald June Perry fought for the batting title the entire season. He ended up fifth with Tony Gwynn copping the trophy at .313.

7. Perry served as the hitting coach for a bunch of teams, including the M's, Pirates, A's, Cubs, Pawtucket Red Sox, Erie SeaWolves, and the USA team in the 2013 World Baseball Classic.

8. Robert Fick, a former child actor, played for Atlanta in 2003. In 1999, he got the final hit in the final game at Tiger Stadium which was the 11,111th homer in the venerable venue.

9. Earl Torgeson, also called "the Earl of Snohomish" (Washington), drew 119 and 102 walks as a Brave in 1950 and 1952, respectively. As a White Sox pinch-hitter, he walked when Chicago scored 11 runs in one inning on one hit against the Royals.

10. Francisco Cabrera blasted one that changed Braves history. On August 21, 1991, his home run in the ninth tied the Reds; Atlanta won in the 13th and reached the World Series, only to lose a nail-biter to the Twins.

CHAPTER 11:

WHO'S GOT SECOND?

QUIZ TIME!

1. Beaneater second baseman Bobby Lowe was the first major-leaguer to hit four homers in a game. He tied and set other records, including total bases in a game. How many?

   a. 13
   b. 15
   c. 17
   d. 19

2. In 1889, Boston signed Lowe from the Milwaukee Brewers for $800 in "one of baseball's biggest bargains." He was one of only three players to participate in all five Beaneater pennants.

   a. True
   b. False

3. Rabbit Maranville batted cleanup in 1914, despite his measly average. The Braves went on to sweep the

powerful Philadelphia A's in the Series. What was Rabbit's batting average?

a. .238
b. .246
c. .255
d. .262

4. Known as one of baseball's most notorious clowns, Rabbit didn't let up as manager. In one of the Cubs' worst seasons (1925), what did he do to his players to stress his authority?

a. He dumped water on sleeping players' heads on a train.
b. He lit a bonfire with his players' bats.
c. He refused to allow players a day off until they won five straight.
d. He withheld players' pay until they dramatically improved.

5. Red Schoendienst spent most of his career with the Cards. Traded in 1957, he helped secure Milwaukee's one championship. Who caught Schoendienst's 1958 fly for the Yankees to end the Braves' dreams of a second World Series win?

a. Bobby Del Greco
b. Joe DiMaggio
c. Mickey Mantle
d. Enos Slaughter

6. Red's fielding percentage (.993) in 1956 stood for 30 years. Who broke his record?

    a. Buddy Bell
    b. Brook Jacoby
    c. Ryne Sandberg
    d. Ozzie Smith

7. In 2003, Marcus Giles suffered a concussion, forcing him to miss the All-Star Game. He came roaring back to break the Braves' record for doubles in a season. How many?

    a. 35
    b. 41
    c. 49
    d. 54

8. Glenn Hubbard took some good-natured kidding from announcers Joe Garagiola and Vin Scully in the 1983 All-Star Game for wearing something uncommon at the time. What was it?

    a. A full beard
    b. A Fu-Manchu mustache
    c. Long sideburns
    d. Numerous gold chains

9. At second base, Hubbard led the Braves in many fielding categories. He was also known as a good _____.

    a. Base stealer
    b. Bunter
    c. Sign stealer
    d. Switch hitter

10. Out of Whitesboro, New York, Mark Lemke decided to skip college to spend four years in Atlanta's minor-league system. Which university did he jump?

    a. Cornell
    b. Princeton
    c. Purdue
    d. SUNY-Purchase

11. In 11 years, Lemke played in four World Series and led all Braves in hitting in the 1991 Fall Classic. What was his average?

    a. .395
    b. .403
    c. .411
    d. .417

12. Félix Millán played second for 12 years for the Braves and the Mets. What was his nickname (translated from Spanish)?

    a. The Cat
    b. The Cobra
    c. The Kitten
    d. The Mustache

13. In 1975, one Atlanta player grounded into a record four double plays all after Félix's four singles. The sad Brave said, "I'd like to thank Félix Millán for making all of this possible." Who was this transgressor?

    a. Dusty Baker
    b. Biff Pocoroba

c. Rowland Office

d. Joe Torre

14. Dan Uggla arrived in Atlanta from Florida after rejecting a $42 million offer. He and Freddie Freeman had simultaneous hitting streaks. How many games did they go?

   a. 17
   b. 20
   c. 23
   d. 27

15. Things got a bit ugly for Uggla in the 2008 All-Star Game. How many errors and strikeouts did he have combined, along with hitting into a double play?

   a. 1/1
   b. 2/2
   c. 3/3
   d. 4/3

16. From Pine Lake, Georgia, Brandon Phillips developed into one of MLB's best second basemen as a Red. His sister, Porsha, played basketball in the WNBA. For which team?

   a. Atlanta Dream
   b. Connecticut Sun
   c. San Antonio Silver Stars
   d. Seattle Storm

17. In 2017, Phillips made a late-season switch to third. Which player's promotion to the Majors was the reason?

a. Ozzie Albies

b. Hunter Renfroe

c. Dansby Swanson

d. Luke Weaver

18. Kelly Johnson recovered from surgery in 2006, spent hours learning to play second base with Coach Hubbard, and became Atlanta's leadoff man. He later lost the spot due to an unacceptable on-base percentage. What was it?

a. .310

b. .325

c. .335

d. .342

19. Johnson platooned at second with Yunel Escobar the same year. When John Schuerholz chose Escobar (who had defected from Cuba), he quipped, "I'm not a _____."

a. Diplomat

b. Dummy

c. Politician

d. Statesman

20. In fact, one of Escobar's best friends and teammates as a kid had already made the Braves squad. Who was the other Cuban who was asked to vouch for Yunel?

a. Yoenis Céspedes

b. Brayan Peña

c. Yasiel Puig

d. Alex Sanchez

QUIZ ANSWERS

1. C – 17

2. B – False, The deal was for $700.

3. B – .246

4. A – He dumped water on sleeping players' heads on a train.

5. C – Mickey Mantle

6. C – Ryne Sandberg

7. C – 49

8. A – A full beard

9. B – Bunter

10. C – Purdue

11. D – .417

12. C – The Kitten

13. D – Joe Torre

14. B – 20 (Uggla topped out at 33 games.)

15. C – 3/3 (Errors/Strikeouts)

16. D – San Antonio Silver Stars

17. A – Ozzie Albies

18. B – .325

19. C – Politician

20. B – Brayan Peña

DID YOU KNOW?

1. NL manager Charlie Manuel selected utility man Omar Infante for the All-Star Team in 2010. He was one of six Braves on the squad that year.

2. An Atlanta native, James Gordon Beckham III led the University of Georgia to the 2008 College World Series. He set the record for home runs (51) at his school's Foley Field in his last home game.

3. Charlie Culberson grew up a Braves fan and, after a stint with the Dodgers, finally came home to play with Atlanta in 2018. Charlie's dad played five minor-league seasons with the Giants, and his granddad's first cousin Leon was a big-leaguer.

4. Culberson's success in the 2018 campaign gained him the nickname "Charlie Clutch."

5. Quilvio Veras led the NL with 56 stolen bags in his rookie season (1995). He had to leave a game in 1998 due to his brother's murder in the Dominican Republic.

6. When Félix Mantilla and Hank Aaron joined the 1953 Jacksonville Braves in the South Atlantic League, they were one of the first two integrated teams in the South.

7. Jeff Treadway clubbed three homers off three different pitchers on May 28, 1990, when the Phils retired Mike Schmidt's number in Veterans Stadium.

8. In 1998, when the Braves won a team-record 106 games, Keith Lockhart split duties at second with Tony Graffanino.

9. Lockhart was almost a hero against the rival Mets in Game 5 of the 1999 NLCS when he entered the game and smacked an RBI triple in the 15th inning. Somehow, New York bounced back to win.

10. Traded to Milwaukee for Bill Bruton, Matt Bolling led NL second basemen in fielding in 1961, 1962, and 1964. Playing with brother Milt in Detroit, they became one of only four sets of brothers to handle the "keystone combination" in MLB history.

CHAPTER 12:

WHO'S AT THE HOT CORNER?

QUIZ TIME!

1. Born in Texarkana, Texas, Eddie Mathews moved with his family to California as a youngster. Which city's high school field is named after him?

   a. Santa Barbara

   b. Santa Cruz

   c. Santa Monica

   d. Santa Rosa

2. When Mathews was battering balls for the Braves in 1954, one famous player said, "I've only known three or four perfect swings in my time. This lad has one of them." Who was it?

   a. Yogi Berra

   b. Ty Cobb

   c. Stan Musial

   d. Ted Williams

3. Bob Elliott, "Mr. Team," won the MVP as a Boston Brave in 1947. Who did he join as the second big-league third baseman with five seasons of 100 RBI?

   a. Art Devlin
   b. Heinie Groh
   c. Willie Kamm
   d. Pie Traynor

4. When the Braves won the pennant in 1948, Elliott led the Majors with 131 walks. What was the previous team record set by Billy Hamilton in 1896?

   a. 100
   b. 110
   c. 125
   d. 130

5. Before becoming a fiery manager, Bobby Cox wasn't able to make the Dodgers. However, he did appear as a player for the Braves before his trade to the Yanks.

   a. True
   b. False

6. Joe Torre is the only major-leaguer to end up with more than 2,000 hits as a player and more than 2,000 wins as a manager. What was his final hit tally?

   a. 2,001
   b. 2,111
   c. 2,252
   d. 2,342

7. Darrell Evans had two stints with the Braves and became the oldest player to lead the MLB in homers. How old was he?

    a. 34
    b. 36
    c. 38
    d. 41

8. Baseball historian Bill James called Evans "the most underrated player in baseball history." Which of the following did he NOT achieve?

    a. Hit 400 homers
    b. Hit at least 100 homers with three different teams
    c. Walk 1,605 times
    d. Win two World Series

9. Braves third baseman Bob Horner said, "When we see people as losers, we treat them with contempt. When we see them as lost, we treat them with _____."

    a. Compassion
    b. Disdain
    c. Love
    d. Pity

10. How many times did Terry Pendleton make it to the World Series in his career without winning?

    a. 2
    b. 4
    c. 5
    d. 7

11. The Cards were so impressed by Terry's development as a third baseman at Louisville in 1984 that they traded their regular hot-corner man to the Braves. Who was he?

    a. Tucker Ashford
    b. Skeeter Barnes
    c. Ken Oberkfell
    d. Andy Van Slyke

12. Terry helped Atlanta climb from sixth place to first and a pennant in his first year as a Brave (1991). Which other key infielder did Schuerholz sign at the same time?

    a. Jeff Blauser
    b. Sid Bream
    c. Tom Herr
    d. Otis Nixon

13. Atlanta bought Vinny Castilla from the Mexican club Saltillo. Which team chose him in the 1992 Expansion Draft?

    a. Arizona
    b. Colorado
    c. Florida
    d. Tampa Bay

14. José "Joey Bats" Bautista became the first player ever to appear on five big-league rosters in the same year (1995). Which of the following was NOT one of the teams?

    a. Baltimore
    b. Kansas City

c. Seattle

d. Tampa Bay

15. In 2015, Juan Uribe was traded to the Braves by the Dodgers in the midst of a three-game set between the teams in Los Angeles. He appeared in his new uniform in the third game, going 0-3, helping Atlanta win.

a. True

b. False

16. Chipper Jones was Atlanta's principal third baseman from 1995 to 2012. What other position did he play in 2002 and 2003?

a. Left field

b. Right field

c. Second base

d. Shortstop

17. Jones has the most career RBI for a third baseman and ranks third on the all-time Braves homer list. Which of the following sluggers is NOT ahead of him?

a. Hank Aaron

b. Eddie Mathews

c. Dale Murphy

18. Joe Torre followed in his brother's footsteps when he signed with Milwaukee as an amateur free agent in 1959. What was this brother's name?

a. Frank

b. Roberto

c. Rocco

d. Tony

19. When Torre feuded over salary with Braves GM Paul Richards before the 1969 season, he was soon traded to the Cards for the 1967 MVP. Who was that?

a. Dick Allen

b. Orlando Cepeda

c. Roberto Clemente

d. Ron Santo

20. Johan Camargo was born in 1993 in Panama. His parents named him after a famous person. Who was his namesake?

a. Bach

b. Cruyff

c. Neeskens

d. Strauss

QUIZ ANSWERS

1. A – Santa Barbara

2. B – Ty Cobb

3. D – Pie Traynor

4. B – 110

5. B – False

6. D – 2,342

7. C – 38

8. D – Win two World Series

9. A – Compassion

10. C – 5

11. C – Ken Oberkfell

12. B – Sid Bream

13. B – Colorado

14. C – Seattle

15. A – True

16. A – Left field

17. C – Dale Murphy

18. A – Frank

19. B – Orlando Cepeda

20. B – Cruyff

DID YOU KNOW?

1. In 2011, José Bautista established a program designed to help Dominican athletes attend American universities.

2. Asked about his trade from Los Angeles to Atlanta, Juan Uribe quipped, "I would've felt bad if they traded me to a soccer, basketball, or football team. But it's another baseball team so I'm happy."

3. Josh Donaldson made contact with the lowest percentage (76.6) of pitches he swung at in the strike zone of all NL batters in 2019.

4. Not only was he "clutch," but Charlie Culberson also agreed to change uniform numbers (from 16 to 8) when Brian McCann returned to Atlanta as a 2019 free agent.

5. Chipper Jones stands alone with Barry Bonds and Carl Yastrzemski as the only players with 400 homers, 2,700 hits, 1,600 RBI, 1,500 walks, and 150 stolen bases.

6. When comparing Jones and Eddie Mathews as the best Braves third bagger ever, consider that Eddie started at 20 years old, while Chipper began at 23 due to a knee injury.

7. Continuing the comparison, the Braves went to the playoffs twice with Mathews, while they managed 12 postseason appearances in a span of 18 years with Jones.

8. In the 1960s, Mathews competed directly with other greats at the hot corner like the Orioles' Brooks Robinson, and the Boyer brothers, Clete and Ken.

9. Bob Elliott helped the 1948 Braves get to the Series and was an All-Star in three of his five Boston seasons.

10. Chipper Jones took time during his Hall of Fame acceptance speech to thank Terry Pendleton for his mentorship.

CHAPTER 13:

WHO'S AT SHORT?

QUIZ TIME!

1. Herman Long played shortstop for the Boston Beaneaters and holds the all-time record for most errors at the position. Which of the following teams did he NOT play for?

    a. Detroit Tigers
    b. Kansas City Cowboys
    c. New York Highlanders
    d. Washington Senators

2. One of the reasons for Long's high error rate was the average number of errors committed by teams per game at the turn of the century was very high. What was that average?

    a. 8
    b. 9
    c. 10
    d. 12

3. Johnny Logan was signed by the Boston Braves in 1947 and cracked a bloop single as the first batter faced by a future Hall-of-Famer in his first mound appearance. Who was it?

   a. Bob Feller
   b. Bubba Harris
   c. Sandy Koufax
   d. Bob Lemon

4. When Travis Jackson was set to succeed Dave Bancroft as the New York Giants shortstop in 1923, manager John McGraw traded the latter to the Braves as a player-manager. Which GM did the trade help?

   a. Miller Huggins
   b. Christy Mathewson
   c. Branch Rickey
   d. Wilbert Robinson

5. Cuban Adeiny Hechavarria defected to Mexico on a boat with 11 others in 2009. What is his older brother's name?

   a. Alan
   b. Alien
   c. Allen
   d. Altuve

6. Dansby Swanson was born in Kennesaw, Georgia, in 1994 to parents Cooter and Nancy. He played collegiate ball at Vanderbilt. What's the name of the university's teams?

   a. Commodores
   b. Continentals

c. Cormorants

d. Cougars

7. In 2016, Swanson was the second Brave ever to hit an inside-the-park homer as his first career round-tripper. Who was the first?

a. Gordon Beckham

b. Rabbit Maranville

c. Paul Runge

d. Jerry Royster

8. After Jeff Blauser retired, which Braves affiliate did he manage in 2006?

a. Danville

b. Gwinnett Stripers

c. Mississippi

d. Rome

9. Rafael Furcal grew up in the Dominican Republic. His father was a taxi driver and an outstanding outfielder. How much did the Braves offer Rafael as an amateur free agent in 1996?

a. $2,500

b. $5,000

c. $10,000

d. $20,000

10. Which Braves shortstop was injured, allowing Furcal to make a jump to the Majors at the start of the 2000 season?

a. José Reyes

b. Jimmy Rollins

c. Miguel Tejada

d. Walt Weiss

11. When Rafael pulled off the 12th unassisted triple play in MLB history in 2003, which St. Louis catcher (who later became Furcal's manager) did he nab at second?

a. Sandy Alomar

b. Joe Girardi

c. Paul Lo Duca

d. Mike Matheny

12. Smooth-fielding Rafael Ramírez played in Atlanta in the 1980s. How many straight years did he lead NL shortstops in double plays?

a. 3

b. 4

c. 5

d. 7

13. At which college did the Braves find Andrelton Simmons when he was drafted in 2010?

a. Boston

b. Dartmouth

c. Western Oklahoma State

d. Wichita State

14. In the 2013 NL Wild Card Game, Simmons hit what appeared to be an eighth-inning single, but it was ruled an infield fly. Fans littered the field with trash. How long was the delay before the Braves finally lost?

a. 5 minutes

b. 10 minutes

c. 19 minutes

d. 27 minutes

15. Bobby Cox said the following of shortstop Yunel Escobar in 2017: "He's a _____ type of player and hitter."

a. Happy-go-lucky

b. No-fear

c. No-nonsense

d. Relaxed

16. Due partially to Escobar's emergence as a top short, the Braves traded starter Édgar Rentería. "Rentería is like a father to him. Rentería taught him a lot," said pal Brayan Peña.

a. True

b. False

17. In 2010, Escobar was traded to Toronto for Álex González. Which other player went north with Yunel?

a. Gregor Blanco

b. Martín Prado

c. Jo-Jo Reyes

d. Billy Wagner

18. When Rabbit Maranville returned to play short for the Braves at age 37, he was still respected for his defensive ability. How many times was he in the top 20 of MVP voting after his return?

a. 2

b. 4

c. 5

d. 7

19. Rafael Furcal had the green light to steal in 2000. His final tally of stolen bags in his first year was the best for rookies since 1914. How many did he grab?

a. 18

b. 25

c. 36

d. 40

20. Since the defensive runs saved stat became available in 2003, this Braves shortstop boasts three of the six highest totals. Who was he?

a. Johan Camargo

b. Josh Donaldson

c. Rafael Furcal

d. Andrelton Simmons

QUIZ ANSWERS

1. D – Washington Senators

2. C – 10

3. C – Sandy Koufax

4. B – Christy Mathewson

5. B – Alien

6. A – Commodores

7. C – Paul Runge

8. C – Mississippi

9. B – $5,000

10. D – Walt Weiss

11. D – Mike Matheny

12. B – 4

13. C – Western Oklahoma State

14. C – 19 minutes

15. B – No-fear

16. A – True

17. C – Jo-Jo Reyes

18. B – 4

19. D – 40

20. D – Andrelton Simmons

DID YOU KNOW?

1. In terms of weighted runs created plus (wRC+), Jeff Blauser is mentioned in the same breath as Hall-of-Famer Barry Larkin of the Reds.

2. Alvin Dark, affectionately known as "the Swamp Fox," was the Braves' shortstop and MLB Rookie of the Year in 1948 with a sparkling .322 BA.

3. Dark played a vital part in the Braves' unlikely run to the World Series, though he batted only .167 in the ultimate loss to Cleveland. Traded to the New York Giants in '49, he was immediately named captain by Leo "The Lip" Durocher, and he had several great seasons in the Big Apple.

4. Denis Menke played shortstop in Milwaukee and accompanied the team in its move to Atlanta. He was part of the so-called "most lopsided trade" in MLB history when he, Joe Morgan, César Gerónimo, and Jack Billingham all went to Cincinnati from Houston.

5. Rabbit Maranville had a lengthy career and showed his durability. "I've spent more time in hospitals than some fellows ever spend in church," he quipped.

6. Maranville once claimed to be the talk of the town for his peculiar way of catching a fly ball: "They later named it the 'vest-pocket catch.'"

7. Even if Dansby Swanson's not hitting on the diamond, he dates soccer star Mallory Pugh, a star of the U.S. Women's National Team and New Jersey's Sky Blue FC.

8. In August 2019, Atlanta signed 30-year-old Adeiny Hechavarria to play short due to Swanson's injury and Camargo's inability to connect. "It's hard to find a legit shortstop this time of year," manager Brian Snitker lamented.

9. Édgar Rentería started 2006 with a 23-game hitting streak (24 counting his last game in 2005), the longest since Ron LeFlore began 1976 with a 30-game stretch.

10. On Opening Day in 2007, Rentería bashed two homers, including the game-winner in the tenth, to sink the Phils. He joined Joe Torre and Fred McGriff with two dingers on Opening Day.

CHAPTER 14:

THE OUTFIELD GANG

QUIZ TIME!

1. Before Babe Ruth spent his final year with the Boston Braves in 1935, he considered managing a Yankees farm team. Which one?

   a. Charleston RiverDogs

   b. Newark Bears

   c. Tampa Tarpons

   d. Trenton Thunder

2. On Opening Day in 1935, Boston had Ruth and pulled in 25,000 fans, plus five of the six New England state governors. The Babe accounted for all Boston's runs in the win, and even made a running catch, despite his size and lack of speed.

   a. True

   b. False

3. Hank Aaron is tied with Willie Mays and Stan Musial for the most All-Star Game appearances. How many?

a. 15

b. 18

c. 21

d. 24

4. In 1954, Aaron broke his ankle and decided to change to a luckier uniform number. It turned out to be the number of homers he hit in a year four times, and the number of pitcher Al Dowling who gave up Hank's 715th. What was the number?

a. 37

b. 44

c. 48

d. 52

5. Dale Murphy started as a catcher but made the transition to the outfield. Which was his best year when he won the MVP Award and played in the All-Star Game as well as all of Atlanta's 162 games?

a. 1980

b. 1982

c. 1984

d. 1986

6. When Andruw Jones cranked up his offensive numbers while patrolling Atlanta's outfield grass in 2000, which famous center fielder was he often compared to?

a. Mickey Mantle

b. Willie Mays

c. Duke Snider

d. Mike Trout

7. Jones connected for homers on his first two World Series at-bats, and he joined Gene Tenace as the only players to do so. With which team did Gene win three straight Series?

    a. Oakland A's
    b. Pittsburgh Pirates
    c. San Diego Padres
    d. St. Louis Cardinals

8. Maybe Jason Heyward got some of his ability to judge balls bouncing in the right-field corner from his parents, who met in the Ivy League. In which school did Eugene and Laura hook up?

    a. Cornell
    b. Dartmouth
    c. Princeton
    d. Yale

9. Although Ender Inciarte finished behind another player in defensive WAR (wins above replacement), he still won the 2016 Gold Glove Award. Who was the other outfielder?

    a. Charlie Blackmon
    b. Dexter Fowler
    c. Billy Hamilton
    d. George Springer

10. Deion Sanders won two Super Bowls and appeared in the 1992 Series, making him the only athlete to accomplish that feat. What was his nickname?

a. Dazzling Deion

b. Deion Delight

c. Prime Time

d. Sweet Sanders

11. Ricardo "Rico" Carty was the NL batting champion in 1966 with the Braves. What was his winning batting average?

    a. .346

    b. .356

    c. .366

    d. .372

12. Outfielder David Justice is a member of the Braves Hall of Fame. Who is this hall named after?

    a. Hank Aaron

    b. Ivan Allen Jr.

    c. Bobby Cox

    d. Ted Turner

13. When Dusty Baker faces a challenge, he thinks to himself, "What would ____ have done? What would _____ have done?" What names are missing?

    a. Hank/Jackie

    b. Grandma/Grandpa

    c. Martin/Jesus

    d. Mom/Dad

14. Marquis Grissom came to the Braves from the Expos when they struggled financially after the 1994 strike. Grissom

caught the last out as the Braves won the '95 World Series. Who was the batter?

a. Carlos Baerga
b. Albert Belle
c. Kenny Lofton
d. Omar Vizquel

15. From Venezuela, Martín Prado came to Atlanta in 2001 as a non-drafted free agent. How did he teach himself English?

a. Cartoons
b. Film subtitles
c. In the clubhouse
d. Riding the Atlanta buses

16. Michael Bourn played Little League in Houston on a team that featured Carl Crawford and was coached by his dad. At age 10, how fast was the pitching Bourn's father made him face in the batting cage?

a. 75 mph
b. 80 mph
c. 85 mph
d. 90 mph

17. After Ron Gant's playing career ended, he moved smoothly into TV. What was the name of the show he co-hosted?

a. *Good Day Atlanta*
b. *Good Morning America*

c. *Peach Tree State Review*

d. *Peach Tree Tales*

18. When Gant entered the "30-30 Club" (30 stolen bases and 30 homers) for the second straight year in 1991, he joined elite company. Which of the following did NOT duplicate the feat?

a. Barry Bonds

b. Bobby Bonds

c. Chipper Jones

d. Willie Mays

19. Ryan Klesko's slugging percentage left him fourth on the all-time Braves list, even ahead of slugger Eddie Mathews. What was Ryan's number?

a. .504

b. .515

c. .525

d. .540

20. From Monroe, Louisiana, Ralph Garr batted .585 for Grambling State University before joining the Braves in 1968. What was Grambling's record in Garr's last year?

a. 36-0

b. 35-1

c. 34-2

d. 32-4

QUIZ ANSWERS

1. B – Newark Bears

2. A – True

3. D – 24

4. B – 44

5. B – 1982

6. B – Willie Mays

7. A – Oakland A's

8. B – Dartmouth

9. C – Billy Hamilton

10. C – Prime Time

11. C – .366

12. B – Ivan Allen Jr.

13. A – Hank (Aaron)/Jackie (Robinson)

14. A – Carlos Baerga

15. B – Film subtitles

16. C – 85 mph

17. A – *Good Day Atlanta*

18. C – Chipper Jones

19. C – .525

20. B – 35-1

DID YOU KNOW?

1. When 53,775 came to see Hammerin' Hank break Ruth's record, Dusty Baker was on deck. After Hank hit one out in the fourth inning, everybody left. "They came to see Hank, not me, not the Braves," Baker mused.

2. Soon after inking one of the richest contracts in Braves history in 1994, Ron Gant broke his leg in an all-terrain vehicle accident and was eventually released.

3. Ralph Garr's speed earned him the nickname "Road Runner." Atlanta went as far as negotiating with Warner Brothers to use cartoon images of the desert bird on the scoreboard.

4. Otis Nixon secured his place in the record books with the most career stolen bases (633) for a player who never made the All-Star Game since its 1933 inception.

5. Lonnie Smith battled drug addiction to become one of baseball's best base stealers in the 1980s. His teams won five pennants and three World Series.

6. One of the NL's top sluggers in the 1930s, Wally Berger of the Braves played in the first All-Star Game in 1933.

7. Ken Griffey Sr. believed his best sports in high school were football, followed by track, and finally baseball.

8. Jeff "Frenchy" Francoeur was known for his strong outfield arm and free-swinging ways at the plate. He was

featured on the *Sports Illustrated* cover as "The Natural" his rookie year (1995).

9. Nick Markakis holds the MLB record for consecutive error-free games as an outfielder, 398.

10. In 2011, Matt Kemp became the first big-leaguer to finish in the top two in both homers and steals since Hank Aaron in 1963.

CHAPTER 15:

THE HEATED RIVALRIES

QUIZ TIME!

1. The Braves' "natural" rivals are located in the East. But when did the Atlanta team win the NL West?

   a. 1965

   b. 1969

   c. 1972

   d. 1975

2. Despite that fine campaign under Lum Harris, the Braves ended up falling to a nemesis in the NLCS that year. Which team stuck it to Atlanta?

   a. Houston

   b. Miracle Mets

   c. St. Louis

   d. Pittsburgh

3. According to various metrics, which team currently has the most "rival points" in terms of Atlanta opponents?

a. New York Mets

b. Philadelphia Phils

c. St. Louis Cards

d. Washington Nats

4. One pundit calls the Phillies the Braves' biggest rivals since their fan base isn't exactly "_____." What word fits?

a. Antagonistic

b. Enamored

c. Endearing

d. Lovable

5. One reason the Washington Nationals are not considered a bigger rival is their "youth" as a franchise. As of 2020, how many years have they been in existence?

a. 8

b. 15

c. 20

d. 23

6. Another reason for fans' dislike of the Phillies is the signing of a particular player in 2019 who rubbed the Braves the wrong way. Who is he?

a. Maikel Franco

b. Bryce Harper

c. Drew Smyly

d. Zack Wheeler

7. Chipper Jones was a Brave throughout his entire 23-year career, yet he named his son "Shea."

a. True

b. False

8. The Braves almost signed a top pitcher (who grew up loving Atlanta's uniforms and hitters) away from the rival Mets. But he ultimately escaped to the Big Apple. Who was it?

a. Cal Koonce

b. Jerry Koosman

c. Nolan Ryan

d. Tom Seaver

9. The series between the Braves and the Phillies is always tough. What's the Atlanta edge in a total of 2,461 games against the City of Brotherly Love?

a. 50

b. 75

c. 99

d. 111

10. The 1999 NLCS saw the Braves sneak past the Mets, only to be swept by the Yanks in the Series. Who was the Mets manager who faced Atlanta's Bobby Cox?

a. Dallas Green

b. George Steinbrenner

c. Joe Torre

d. Bobby Valentine

11. When the Braves bashed the Mets in Shea Stadium just before the 1999 playoffs, Chipper Jones quipped, "Now all

the Mets fans can go home and put on their _____ stuff."
What's missing?

a. Crybaby

b. Stupid

c. Yankees

d. Winter

12. When the '99 NLCS moved to New York, what did Mets fans chant to taunt Jones?

a. "Bonehead Jones!"

b. "Lamer!"

c. "Larry!"

d. "Loser!"

13. If the Braves are linked to the Cincinnati Red Stockings, then their oldest rivals are actually from Chicago. When did that rivalry start?

a. 1870

b. 1888

c. 1895

d. 1905

14. The rivalry between the Braves and Phillies dates back to previous centuries. Who was the Braves manager who did his best to fan the animosity between the two from 1884 to 1890?

a. Charlie Grimm

b. Frank Selee

c. George Stallings

d. Harry Wright

15. When the Boston Braves played a Florida exhibition against the Yankees in 1953, they began the day as Boston and ended it as Milwaukee. Which former Brave had a hit to help New York win?

    a. Don Bollweg
    b. Johnny Mize
    c. Johnny Sain
    d. Warren Spahn

16. In the 1993 NLCS, Philadelphia stunned the 104-win Braves as the Phils went on to their first World Series since 1980. Who was the MVP?

    a. Brad Brink
    b. Lenny Dykstra
    c. John Kruk
    d. Curt Schilling

17. What advantage do the Braves hold over their "ancient" opponents, the Cubs, in terms of pennants?

    a. 16-15
    b. 20-11
    c. 30-15
    d. 19-18

18. When he decided to leave the Cubs in 1992, which team did Greg Maddux snub before becoming a Brave?

    a. Cards
    b. Mets
    c. Phillies
    d. Yankees

19. Who was the Braves' hero in 1999 who drew a bases-loaded walk off the Mets' Kenny Rogers to send Atlanta home as 10-9 winners?

    a. Bret Boone
    b. Javy López
    c. Dave Sheinin
    d. Walt Weiss

20. When the Braves brawled against the San Diego Padres in 1984, how many players were ejected?

    a. 10
    b. 13
    c. 18
    d. 21

QUIZ ANSWERS

1. B – 1969

2. B – Miracle Mets

3. D – Washington Nats

4. C – Endearing

5. B – 15

6. B – Bryce Harper

7. A – True

8. D – Tom Seaver

9. D – 111

10. D – Bobby Valentine

11. C – Yankees

12. C – "Larry!"

13. A – 1870

14. D – Harry Wright

15. C – Johnny Sain

16. D – Curt Schilling

17. A – 16-15

18. D – Yankees

19. C – Dave Sheinin

20. B – 13

DID YOU KNOW?

1. As with many baseball brawls, it started with a beanball. In fact, Braves starter Pascual Pérez plunked Padres leadoff man Alan Wiggins in the very first inning of the August 12, 1984, game. Then San Diego pitchers threw at Pérez every time he came to the plate, eventually leading to an all-out brawl that resulted in a record 17 ejections.

2. The rivalry between the Braves and the Phillies cooled off at the end of the nineteenth century but flared again in 1915 when both teams battled for supremacy in the East.

3. Regarding individual rivalries, who had a leg up, Hank Aaron or Bob Gibson? They faced each other from 1959 to 1975, and Aaron wins in terms of both WAR and ERA/OPS (Though, Chipper Jones nips Aaron on the all-time OPS list.)!

4. Hank Aaron himself wasn't a rival of the great Ruth. Nevertheless, he crushed Babe's record. Vin Scully called it: "A Black man is getting a standing ovation in the Deep South for breaking a record of an all-time baseball idol."

5. Tris Speaker had enough trouble as a Ty Cobb rival, and now he's being compared to Aaron. Hank wins out, seven offensive categories to four for Tris.

6. Some say, "A hated rival should not be celebrated." Yet Mets management decided to honor Chipper Jones in 2012 despite the fact that he "owned" Mets pitching for years.

7. When Minnesota agreed to pay Josh $92 million, GM Alex Anthopoulos said, "I never want to see teams in our division get better. Josh Donaldson makes everybody better. From a selfish standpoint, because I know how great a player he is, I'd rather he's in the American League than the NL."

8. Some hoped the 2019 Braves would make a playoff run past the Cardinals, Dodgers, and Yankees—all teams that caused "some amount of sadness" to the Braves in the past.

9. In the 1996 NLCS, the Braves had their backs to the proverbial wall against the Cards. But they won three straight, outscoring St. Louis by 32-1.

10. Want to know your rivals? Look at their literature. Some Astros backers consider the Braves one of their biggest rivals; especially in the 1990s, when Atlanta shut down Houston three times in a four-year span.

CONCLUSION

The great names roll off your tongue: Chipper Jones, Rabbit Maranville, Bobby Cox, Glavine, Maddux, and Smoltz, Spahn and Sain and pray for rain, and perhaps the greatest hitter of all time, Hammerin' Hank Aaron, the mighty man who smashed 755 career homers.

This is it: an amazing collection of Braves information, statistics, and trivia at your fingertips! Regardless of how you fared on the quizzes, we hope you found this book entertaining, enlightening, and educational.

Ideally, you knew many of these details already but also learned a great deal more about the history of the Braves, their players, coaches, managers, and some of the quirky stories surrounding the team, its history, and its special ballparks. If you got a little peek into the colorful details that make being a fan so much more enjoyable, then our mission was accomplished!

The good news is that the trivia doesn't have to stop there. Spread the word. Challenge your fellow Braves fans to see if they can do any better. Share some of the stories with the next generation to help them become Braves supporters, too.

If you're a big enough Atlanta fan, consider creating your own quiz with some of the details you know weren't presented here. Then test your friends to see if they can match your knowledge.

The Braves are one of baseball's most storied franchises with a long history, many stretches of success, and a few that were a bit less successful. They've had glorious superstars, iconic moments, and hilarious tales. Most of all, they have wonderful, passionate fans. Thank you for being one of them. "For the A."